PATRICK H. PERRINE

Conquering the Globe

Navigating Success through Strategic Global Entrepreneurship

First published by AMZ Publishing / KDP 2024

This book has been created with the assistance of artificial intelligence tools. The insights, recommendations, and content generated have undergone review and modification by human experts but inherently possess the characteristics and limitations of AI-generated content.

While every effort has been made to ensure accuracy, comprehensiveness, and relevance, the content may not be free from errors, omissions, or subjectivity. The author and publisher disclaim any warranties, express or implied, as to the completeness, accuracy, or suitability of the content for any specific purpose. Readers are advised to use this book as a guide, complemented by their own research, judgment, and professional advice where appropriate.

Neither the author, publisher, nor the AI providers assume any liability or responsibility for any loss, damage, or adverse outcomes resulting from the application of any of the information, techniques, or methods presented in this book. It's the reader's responsibility to be aware of current industry standards, best practices, and regulatory requirements in their respective fields or business endeavors.

First edition

ISBN: 9798884648241

This book was professionally typeset on Reedsy.
Find out more at reedsy.com

DEDICATION

To you, the relentless dreamer and dauntless doer, embarking on a journey across the vast expanse of global entrepreneurship. May this book serve as your compass, guiding your vision and illuminating your path. Here's to the audacity of your aspirations, the courage in your steps, and the legacy you will etch upon the world. Dive in, conquer, and may your story inspire the chapters of those who follow.

Warmly,
Patrick

"There is no passion to be found playing small—in settling for a life that is less than the one you are capable of living."

— NELSON MANDELA

Contents

Preface   viii

Be A Unicorn: The New Entrepreneur's Ulti-
mate Guide To...   x

I   Part One

1   The Evolving Landscape of Entrepreneurship   3
Opening Anecdote: Automattic's Global Footprint   4
Case Study Highlight: Patagonia - Pio-
neering Sustainability in Business   6
   Exercise: Global Entrepreneurship Workshop   7
2   Cultivating the Mindset of a Successful Entrepreneur   10
Opening Anecdote: The Rowling Resilience   11
Case Study Highlight: Canva - Melanie
Perkins' Journey from Yearbook Design
to Billion-Dollar Unicorn   13
   Exercise: Entrepreneurial Mindset
   Mastery Workshop   14
3   Building on Ideas: From Ideation to Opportunity   17
Opening Anecdote: A Pebble's Rise and Lesson   17
Case Study Highlight: Beyond Meat -
Plant-Based Revolution in the Meat In-
dustry   20

Exercise Workshop: From Ideation to
Opportunity Workshop   21
4 Crafting the Edge: Navigating Market
   Dynamics & Distinction   24
Opening Anecdote: The Story Behind
LEGO's Reinvention   25
Case Study Highlight: Duolingo - Gami-
fying Language Learning   27
   Exercise: Market Dynamics & Distinc-
   tion Workshop   28
5 Harnessing the Power of Business
   Model Innovation   31
Opening Anecdote: Rethinking Glasses:
The Zenni Optical Story   32
Case Study Highlight: Warby Parker -
Disrupting the Eyewear Monopoly   33
   Exercise: Harnessing the Power of Busi-
   ness Model Innovation Workshop   34
6 Building a Strong Startup Team   37
Opening Anecdote: Spotify - Unifying a
Global Team: 38
Case Study Highlight: Atlassian: Diver-
sity as a Strength   43
   Exercise: Team Dynamics Mastery Workshop   44

II   Part Two

7 Strategic Planning and Goal Setting   49
Opening Anecdote: The Strategic Leap of
Spanx by Sara Blakely   50

Case Study Highlight: GreenLeaf Innovations - Revolutionizing Agri-tech for
Small-Scale Farmers   53
    Exercise: Strategic Planning and Goal
    Setting Workshop   55
8   Product Development and Innovation   58
  Opening Anecdote: The Dyson Vacuum Revolution   58
  Case Study Highlight: Raspberry Pi -
Empowering Global Education Through
Innovation   61
    Exercise: Product Innovation and Development Workshop   62
9   Crafting a Memorable Brand - The Soul
    of Your Startup   66
  Opening Anecdote: The Sweet Success of
Ben & Jerry's   66
    Building a Strong Brand Identity and Positioning   67
    Developing a Marketing Plan   67
  Case Study Highlight: Chobani - Revolutionizing the Yogurt Industry with Purpose   69
    Exercise: Brand Essence Workshop   70
10   Sales and Customer Acquisition - Crafting a Growth Blueprint   74
  Opening Anecdote: The Dominance of
Zoom in a Pandemic World   75
    Entrepreneurship in Action: Key Ingredients   77
  Case Study Highlight: HubSpot's Revolution in Sales and Marketing   78
    Exercise: Sales and Customer Acquisition Mastery Workshop   80
11   Scalability and Growth Strategies   83

Opening Anecdote: How Etsy Crafted its Niche 83
Case Study Highlight: Zoom's Meteoric
Rise in Digital Communication 86
Exercise: Growth and Scalability Action Plan Workshop 87
12 Financial Management and Funding 91
Opening Anecdote: Amazon's Growth Trajectory 91
Case Study Highlight: Palantir's Financial
Strategy: Harnessing Data for Stability 94
Exercise: Financial Mastery Workshop 96

III Part Three

13 Leading Distributed Teams 101
Opening Anecdote: The Success Secrets
of Basecamp 101
Case Study Highlight: GitLab's All-Remote Culture 104
Exercise: Distributed Leadership Mastery Workshop 105
14 Building a Culture of Innovation 108
Opening Anecdote: How Adobe Pivoted
to Subscription 109
Case Study Highlight: The Continuous
Innovation at 3M 111
Exercise: Innovation Culture Workshop 112
15 Mastering Remote Team Management 115
Opening Anecdote: The Story Behind
Notion's Success 116
Case Study Highlight: The All-Remote
Ethos of Buffer 119

Exercise: Remote Team Mastery Workshop 120
16 Performance Management and Feedback 122
Opening Anecdote: Indra Nooyi's Leadership at PepsiCo 123
Case Study Highlight: Intuit's Embrace of Continuous Feedback for Remote Workforce Growth 126
Exercise: Performance Management and Feedback Workshop 128
17 Conflict Resolution and Team Dynamics 131
Opening Anecdote: LinkedIn's Evolutionary Growth Story 132
Case Study Highlight: Asana's Holistic Approach to Team Harmony 135
Exercise: Team Dynamics and Conflict Resolution Workshop 137

IV Part Four

18 Taking Calculated Leaps - Risk and Uncertainty 143
Opening Anecdote: Toyota's Leap into Hybrid Technology 144
Case Study Highlight: Dropbox - From Backup Solution to Synchronization Titan 147
Exercise: Risk Management Workshop 148
19 Crisis Management and Business Continuity 151
Opening Anecdote: The Resilience of BlackBerry 152
Case Study Highlight: The Transformation of Nokia 155
Exercise: Crisis Management and Business Continuity Workshop 156

20 Embracing Innovation and Disruption   159

Opening Anecdote: The Rise and Fall of Kodak   159

Case Study Highlight: Ayah Bdeir and littleBits - Democratizing Hardware Innovation   162

Exercise: Innovation and Disruption Workshop   164

21 Leveraging Data and Analytics for Startups   167

Opening Anecdote: The Analytics Powerhouse: SAS   168

Case Study Highlight: Sheila Lirio Marcelo and Care.com - Harnessing Data to Connect Families and Caregivers   171

Exercise: Data Mastery Workshop for Startups   173

22 Navigating Regulatory and Legal Considerations   175

Opening Anecdote: Sheryl Sandberg, COO of Facebook   176

Case Study Highlight: Jessica O. Matthews and Uncharted Power - Revolutionizing Energy through Innovation   179

Exercise: Legal and Regulatory Readiness Workshop   181

V   Part Five

23 Sustainable Business Practices   187

Opening Anecdote: The Ethical Coffee Supply Chain of Starbucks   188

Crafting a Sustainable Business Strategy: 188

Case Study Highlight: Ecosia - The Search Engine Planting Trees   190

Exercise: Sustainability Integration Workshop   191

24 Entrepreneurial Ethics and Corporate
     Social Responsibility   193
     Opening Anecdote: The Green Energy
     Pursuits of IKEA   194
     Case Study Highlight: Blake Mycoskie
     and TOMS Shoes - Buy One, Give One   196
        Exercise: Ethical and CSR Strategy Workshop   197
25 Crafting the Grand Finale - Exit Strate-
     gies and Leaving a...   200
     Opening Anecdote: The Visionary
     Legacy of Steve Jobs at Apple   201
     Case Study Highlight: Janice Bryant
     Howroyd and ACT-1 Group - Pioneering
     Workforce Solutions with Integrity   203
        Exercise: Legacy Planning Workshop   205

Epilogue: Unleashing the Extraordinary   208
The Ask   212
About the Author   213
Also by Patrick H. Perrine   216

Preface

As you embark on the global stage of entrepreneurship, where the vastness of opportunity is matched only by the complexity of challenges, 'Conquering the Globe' stands as your indispensable guide. This volume, integral to the 'Be A Unicorn: The New Entrepreneur's Ultimate Guide to Success' series, is meticulously crafted as the companion workbook to Step 2 of 'Unicorn Rising: Strategic Entrepreneurship: Steering Success in the Global Landscape.'

In my quest to demystify the journey of turning a vision into a global phenomenon, 'Conquering the Globe' was conceived. It's more than a narrative; it's a workbook that translates the lofty ideals of global entrepreneurship into actionable plans and strategies. Each chapter, inspired by the corresponding section in 'Unicorn Rising,' is designed to propel you from theory to practice, equipping you with the tools necessary to navigate the global business landscape.

Through the lens of pioneering brands and innovative startups, this book explores the essence of global entrepreneurship—not as an abstract concept, but as a tangible, navigable path. Beyond inspiration, 'Conquering the Globe' provides you with a practical framework, from understanding international market dynamics to executing cross-border strategies effectively.

Embrace this book as your mentor and roadmap, guiding

you through the intricacies of establishing and expanding your venture across borders. It's a journey of discovery, learning, and, most importantly, applying the principles of global entrepreneurship with confidence and precision.

As 'Conquering the Globe' accompanies you on this venture, remember that the journey of global entrepreneurship is a testament to human creativity and resilience. It's your passion, vision, and unwavering commitment to innovation that will define your success on the international stage. Together, let us set sail towards uncharted territories, armed with the wisdom of 'Unicorn Rising' and the strategic insights of 'Conquering the Globe.' Here's to conquering not just markets, but hearts and minds across the globe.

Be A Unicorn: The New Entrepreneur's Ultimate Guide To Success

Dream It, Build It:
An Aspirational Odyssey Through
Entrepreneurship in Ten Inspiring Volumes.

Volume Two

CONQUERING THE GLOBE
Navigating Success through Strategic Global
Entrepreneurship

I

Part One

Foundational Elements of Startup Strategy

1

The Evolving Landscape of Entrepreneurship

"Change is the only constant in life."
— Heraclitus

A fter setting the foundations in "Unicorn Rising," you're now poised on the cusp of a thrilling adventure. "Conquering the Globe: Navigating Success through Strategic Global Entrepreneurship" is your compass, illuminating the vast and exhilarating realm of global entrepreneurship. As we delve into the second volume of the "Be A Unicorn Series," we beckon you into an odyssey of ambition and vision that transcends geographical boundaries.

Every entrepreneur, much like an intrepid explorer, has aspirations to chart unknown territories, to make their mark on the world. It's this universal aspiration that is the beating heart of global entrepreneurship. But as with any journey, the path to international success is strewn with challenges, unfamiliar terrains, and the need for strategic navigation.

This is not just another book—it's an immersive experience,

designed to transform your vision into a worldwide venture. As we journey through its pages, we'll tread the footsteps of pioneering entrepreneurs, extracting wisdom from their tales and learning from their triumphs and tribulations. The narratives within offer not just guidance but a clarion call, urging you to take bold strides, to harness the electrifying synergy of technology and interconnectedness, and to etch your indelible footprint on the global stage.

So, as you stand at this threshold, remember: every chapter, every anecdote, every lesson here is a beacon. Whether you're plotting your first voyage or are a seasoned navigator of the global entrepreneurial seas, "Conquering the Globe" is crafted to be your trusted companion, a lodestar in your audacious quest to transform dreams into international victories.

Are you ready, dear reader? Take a deep breath, embrace the thrill of anticipation, and let's set forth on this grand expedition of strategic global entrepreneurship.

Opening Anecdote: Automattic's Global Footprint

Automattic, the company behind WordPress, took a road less traveled by building a completely distributed team. The benefits were clear: access to global talent and 24-hour productivity. But the challenges, like communication and cultural nuances, demanded unique solutions. This choice captures the modern entrepreneurial essence: leveraging technology, breaking boundaries, and evolving continuously.

Navigating Modern Entrepreneurship: The Impact of Technology

Technology's disruptive force has heralded opportunities

and reshaped industries. From AI chatbots to blockchain's promise in supply chain management, technology has democratized access to resources and global networks.

The Rise of Distributed and Global Teams

Gone are the days when startups were rooted to a single location. Distributed teams span time zones, bringing diverse talent to the table. Yet, this global approach needs careful coordination and seamless communication.

The Changing Expectations of the Modern Entrepreneur

Today's entrepreneurs seek more than profit. Purpose-driven ventures and an emphasis on diversity and inclusion highlight a paradigm shift towards holistic success.

> *Quick Thought:*
> *Modern entrepreneurship is a dance with evolution, one where adaptability and foresight lead to success in a dynamic landscape.*

Entrepreneurship in Action: Key Ingredients

- **Technological Agility:** Being receptive to emerging technologies and integrating them effectively is the cornerstone of modern entrepreneurial success.
- **Global Mindset:** In an interconnected world, understanding global markets and cultures can differentiate a venture.
- **Purpose Beyond Profit:** Successful ventures resonate with a deeper purpose, often aligned with societal or environmental positive impacts.

Case Study Highlight: Patagonia - Pioneering Sustainability in Business

Rooted in Climbing: Patagonia's origins trace back to a small company making climbing tools. Founder Yvon Chouinard, an avid climber himself, began by designing reusable climbing equipment, subtly setting the tone for Patagonia's environmental ethos.

Commitment to the Environment: As the company ventured into apparel, their commitment to sustainability became even more evident. Patagonia started experimenting with organic cotton, realizing the harmful impacts of traditional cotton farming on the environment.

1% for the Planet: In an audacious move, Patagonia pledged to donate 1% of their total sales (not just profits) to grassroots environmental groups. This initiative, known as "1% for the Planet," became a benchmark for corporate environmental responsibility, inspiring other companies to follow suit.

Sustainability as a Brand Ethos: Today, Patagonia's brand is synonymous with environmental and ethical responsibility. From promoting fair labor practices to innovative recycling programs for their products, Patagonia has seamlessly woven sustainability into its business fabric. Their journey showcases that profitability and environmental stewardship aren't mutually exclusive but can coexist and even amplify each other. Through continuous innovation, genuine commitment, and transparent communication, Patagonia has not only succeeded in the market but has also set new standards for businesses globally.

```
Pro Tip: The modern entrepreneurial journey is more
than navigating business dynamics. It's about
understanding global shifts, technological trends,
and societal needs to carve a unique path.
```

Exercise: Global Entrepreneurship Workshop

Market Exploration and Strategy Development:

- **Global Market Analysis:** Select three potential global markets for your venture. Conduct a comprehensive analysis of each, focusing on economic conditions, cultural nuances, competitive landscape, and regulatory environment. Determine the viability and strategic entry points for your product or service.
- **Cross-Cultural Engagement Plan:** Develop a plan for engaging with each target market in a culturally sensitive and effective manner. This should include tailored marketing strategies, product localization efforts, and customer service adaptations to meet local expectations and preferences.
- **Technology and Innovation Integration:** Evaluate the role of emerging technologies in supporting your global expansion. Identify specific technologies that can enhance your operational efficiency, customer engagement, or product offering in each target market. Develop a phased plan for integrating these technologies into your business operations.

Building and Managing a Global Team:

- **Designing a Global Team Structure:** Outline an organizational structure that supports your global expansion goals. Identify key roles that need to be filled and the specific skills and experiences required for each. Consider the logistical challenges of managing a distributed team and propose solutions for effective collaboration and communication.
- **Cultural Competency and Training:** Create a comprehensive training program to enhance cultural competency among your team members. Focus on developing skills in cross-cultural communication, negotiation, and leadership to navigate the complexities of global business environments effectively.
- **Leadership for Global Growth:** Plan for the development of global leadership within your organization. Identify potential leaders and design a leadership development program that emphasizes strategic thinking, cultural agility, and the ability to drive growth in diverse markets.

Adaptation and Continuous Improvement:

- **Market Feedback and Adaptation Mechanisms:** Establish systems for collecting and analyzing feedback from each target market. Use this feedback to make informed decisions about product adaptations, marketing strategies, and customer service improvements.
- **Continuous Learning and Development:** Implement a continuous learning culture within your organization focused on global market trends, technological advance-

ments, and competitive strategies. Encourage ongoing education and knowledge sharing among team members to foster innovation and adaptability.

- **Reflective Practice and Strategic Evolution:** Regularly review your global expansion strategy and operational practices. Engage in reflective practices to assess what is working well and identify areas for improvement. Use insights gained from these reflections to iterate and evolve your approach to global entrepreneurship.

Challenge For You: Identify a global trend or shift in consumer behavior that could impact your industry. Develop a strategic initiative that leverages this trend to create new opportunities for your venture.

Are You Ready to Embrace the Evolution? As you embark on the journey of global entrepreneurship, remember that success in today's dynamic business environment requires more than just a great product or service. It demands a strategic approach to global expansion, an unwavering commitment to continuous learning, and the agility to adapt to changing market conditions. With the right strategies and mindset, you can navigate the complexities of the global marketplace and turn your entrepreneurial vision into a reality.

Coming Up Next: Chapter 2 delves deeper into identifying and capitalizing on global opportunities, offering insights and strategies for recognizing untapped markets and understanding the intricacies of global demand. Join us as we explore the next steps in your journey to conquering the globe.

2

Cultivating the Mindset of a Successful Entrepreneur

"In the middle of difficulty lies opportunity."
— Albert Einstein

A s we stand at the precipice of entrepreneurial greatness, we are reminded that the bedrock of any transformative venture is a singular, compelling idea. It is the initial spark that, when fanned into flames, has the potential to illuminate industries, rewrite paradigms, and touch the lives of countless individuals. In this enriching chapter, journey with us into the sanctum of ideation and opportunity recognition, as we chart the landscapes of innovation, unearthing methodologies that not only stimulate creative thought but also discern the very opportunities that stand poised to redefine markets.

Entrepreneurship is a saga of both the known and the unknown, rife with peaks of opportunities and valleys of challenges. Yet, at the core of this tumultuous journey is a mindset. A mindset that isn't just about acknowledging the presence of adversities but skillfully navigating through them, transforming potential pitfalls into milestones of achievement. Together, let's embark on this odyssey, unraveling the essence of the entrepreneurial mindset, dissecting its components, and arming ourselves with the wisdom to cultivate it.

The chronicles of every great product, every revolutionary service, and each disruptive platform share a common origin: an idea. However, this idea, though paramount, is merely the prologue. The narrative's heart pulsates with the entrepreneur's spirit – a beacon of resilience, a testament to risk-taking, and a visionary who, come what may, stays true to their dream. Allow this chapter to be your compass, guiding you through the myriad layers of this mindset, empowering you to realize your potential, tackle uncertainties, and set forth on a trajectory to unparalleled success.

Opening Anecdote: The Rowling Resilience

Before the name J.K. Rowling became emblematic of wizardry and wonder, she was a beacon of determination amidst a sea of adversities. From the confines of welfare to the echoing rejections of multiple publishers, Rowling's journey was an odyssey in resilience. However, instead of being ensnared by despair, she viewed each setback as a catalyst, an invigorating challenge. Today, she stands not merely as an author but as a maverick who transformed a mere idea into a transcendent empire, a testimony to the prowess of the right mindset.

The Psyche of a Pioneering Entrepreneur

- **Overcoming Self-Doubt:** In the corridors of entrepreneurship, the whispers of doubt are incessant. Yet, the key lies not in silencing these murmurs but in channeling them. Transforming these doubts into steely resolve can shift trajectories, converting looming hurdles into landmarks of achievement.

- **Embracing Risk-Taking:** Risk is not a dalliance with recklessness but a dance with vision. True entrepreneurs don't plunge into the abyss; they stride forward, eyes on the horizon, turning adversities into stepping stones.
- **Nurturing Resilience:** In the entrepreneurial realm, setbacks aren't anomalies but inevitabilities. It's the resilience, the unwavering spirit that charts the narrative. A growth mindset, where every setback is an opportunity in disguise, lays the foundation for perennial success.

Quick Thought:
The entrepreneurial mindset isn't a bestowed legacy; it's a meticulously sculpted art. It isn't the eradication of fear but the audacity to march forward, undeterred by it.

Entrepreneurship in Action: Key Ingredients

- **Clear Vision:** Peer deep into the 'why' of your journey. It transcends mere market gaps; it's about aligning these voids with a burning passion.
- **Continuous Learning:** The entrepreneurial cosmos is in perpetual flux. To remain pertinent, one must be like water—adapting, evolving, and learning at every bend.
- **Network Nurturing:** In the entrepreneurial symphony,

your network is the harmonious chorus that amplifies your song. Forge bonds, maintain alliances, and doors you never perceived will swing open.

Case Study Highlight: Canva - Melanie Perkins' Journey from Yearbook Design to Billion-Dollar Unicorn

Perkins' Entrepreneurial Spark: Melanie Perkins, while studying at the University of Western Australia, encountered a challenge that many students faced: creating visually appealing yearbooks. This experience ignited her entrepreneurial spirit, leading her to develop Fusion Books, a startup that streamlined the yearbook creation process, making it both easier and more accessible for students and schools.

The Evolution to Canva: Recognizing the broader application of simplifying graphic design, Perkins envisioned a platform that could democratize design for people regardless of their expertise. This vision catalyzed the expansion from Fusion Books to Canva, an online graphic design tool aimed at making professional-level design accessible to everyone, from businesses to individual users.

Overcoming Challenges: The road to success was fraught with obstacles, from the daunting task of finding a tech partner who shared her vision to the arduous journey of securing funding in a competitive market. Despite these initial hurdles, Canva's intuitive user interface and comprehensive design features quickly captured the market's attention, leading to rapid user growth and widespread adoption.

A Unicorn's Rise: Canva's journey from a nascent startup to a billion-dollar unicorn is a testament to Perkins' foresight, determination, and ability to evolve a simple idea into a global phenomenon. Today, Canva is not just a tool for graphic design but a platform that empowers millions to create, design, and communicate their ideas to the world. Melanie Perkins' story exemplifies the transformative impact of perseverance, innovative thinking, and the power of making complex processes simple and accessible.

```
Pro Tip: Treasure feedback, but remain true to your
vision. Not every voice understands your path, yet
in the orchestra of opinions, some notes can truly
refine your melody.
```

Exercise: Entrepreneurial Mindset Mastery Workshop

Self-Reflection and Growth Mindset:

- **Overcoming Adversity Log:** Reflect on three significant challenges or failures you've encountered in your entrepreneurial journey. For each, jot down the key lessons learned and how these experiences have contributed to your growth mindset. Consider how adopting a different perspective at the time might have altered the outcomes.
- **Risk Evaluation Exercise:** Identify a current or upcoming decision in your venture that involves significant risk. Break down the potential risks and benefits, employing a SWOT analysis (Strengths, Weaknesses, Opportunities, Threats) to gain clarity. Devise a strategy to mitigate identified risks while maximizing the potential benefits.

Vision and Continuous Learning:

- **Vision Board Creation:** Craft a vision board that encapsulates the core mission and aspirations of your startup. Incorporate images, quotes, and symbols that resonate with your entrepreneurial spirit and goals. This board should serve as a daily reminder of your 'why' and inspire continuous momentum.
- **Learning Agenda Planner:** Set up a monthly learning agenda focused on areas where you seek growth or improvement. This could range from mastering new technologies to understanding global market trends. Commit to specific actions, such as completing online courses, attending workshops, or engaging in peer learning sessions.

Networking and Resilience Building:

- **Strategic Networking Plan:** Map out a strategy to expand your entrepreneurial network over the next quarter. Identify key individuals or groups within your industry or related fields that you aim to connect with. Outline the steps you'll take to initiate and nurture these connections, setting clear goals for each relationship.
- **Resilience Reflection Journal:** Start a resilience journal, documenting instances where you faced setbacks or rejections. For each entry, note down your emotional response, coping strategies, and any shifts in perspective or approach that resulted. This exercise is intended to build awareness of your resilience over time and encourage a proactive stance toward challenges.

Challenge For You: Identify an area within your entrepreneurial mindset that you feel needs strengthening—be it risk tolerance, resilience, or vision clarity. Over the next month, focus on activities and practices that enhance this specific area. Set measurable goals to track your progress and reflect on the changes observed in your mindset and decision-making process.

Are You Ready to Cultivate a Powerful Entrepreneurial Mindset? Embracing the mindset of a successful entrepreneur is about more than just determination and hard work; it's about cultivating resilience, embracing continuous learning, and nurturing a vision that drives every action. As you engage with the exercises outlined, you're not just preparing to navigate the entrepreneurial landscape; you're setting the stage for transformative growth and lasting impact.

Coming Up Next: Chapter 3 takes us into the heart of team dynamics and the art of building a cohesive, driven team that shares your vision and passion. Discover strategies for assembling your dream team and fostering an environment where innovation and collaboration flourish.

3

Building on Ideas: From Ideation to Opportunity

"The way to get started is to quit talking and begin doing."
— Walt Disney

A t the heart of every great venture is a spark – a concept, an inspiration. But while ideas are plentiful, the alchemy of transforming them into tangible opportunities is a nuanced dance. In this chapter, we journey through the labyrinth of ideation, showcasing tools, strategies, and insights that can lead visionaries from mere conception to actionable business potential.

Opening Anecdote: A Pebble's Rise and Lesson

When we reminisce about smartwatches, the sophisticated sheen of the Apple Watch might dominate our thoughts. But before its reign, the Pebble smartwatch carved its niche. Emerging as a sensation in 2012 on Kickstarter, Pebble wasn't merely an invention; it was a testament to identifying and tapping into market demand. Crowdfunding contributions exceeded $10 million, proving that the right idea at the right time can create tidal waves. Although Pebble later navigated choppy waters, it remains emblematic of recognizing and seizing market gaps with precision.

The Foundation of Great Ventures

- **Cultivating Ideas:** Every disruptive idea finds its roots in brainstorming, keen observation, or a customer's offhand remark. The avenues are diverse – from assembling eclectic teams to deliberate, to the serendipitous eureka moments upon spotting an emerging trend. Ideation is fluid, demanding both structure and spontaneity.
- **Spotting Gaps and Addressing Needs:** An idea evolves into an opportunity when it resonates, when it offers a solution or satiates a hitherto unaddressed need. Entrepreneurs, armed with market insights and an empathetic understanding of their customer base, are uniquely positioned to decipher these latent demands.
- **Validating Through Research:** The entrepreneurial landscape is littered with the remnants of unchecked assumptions. It's imperative to test waters before diving deep. Whether through comprehensive research methodologies or the real-world testing of MVPs, validation safeguards ventures from avoidable pitfalls.
- **Iterative Excellence:** Evolution is at the heart of entrepreneurship. The voyage from an initial spark to a full-blown opportunity is rife with feedback loops, pivots, and refinements. Successful entrepreneurs are those who listen, adapt, and continually sculpt their vision to

perfection.

Quick Thought:
Embracing change and adaptability can transform entrepreneurial ventures. Stagnation is the enemy; evolution is the ally.

Entrepreneurship in Action: Key Ingredients

- **Diverse Brainstorming:** Ideas thrive in diversity. By bringing together minds from varied backgrounds and experiences, the ideation phase becomes a crucible of innovation.
- **Trend Analysis:** In the age of information, being oblivious to market trends can be detrimental. Staying abreast of shifts not only fuels ideation but also offers competitive advantages.
- **Customer-Centric Ideation:** The most resonant ideas often emanate from customer insights. When entrepreneurs intertwine customer feedback with ideation, the resulting concepts are both innovative and demand-driven.

Case Study Highlight: Beyond Meat - Plant-Based Revolution in the Meat Industry

The Visionary Seed: Ethan Brown founded Beyond Meat with a transformative goal - to challenge the traditional meat industry by offering plant-based alternatives that could satisfy the global appetite for meat without the environmental footprint. This vision was grounded in the belief that technology could bridge the gap between meat lovers and plant-based diets.

Innovation at its Core: Beyond Meat invested heavily in research and development to create groundbreaking products that mimicked the taste, texture, and nutritional value of meat. This relentless pursuit of innovation led to the development of products that appealed not just to vegetarians and vegans but also to omnivores looking for sustainable dietary choices.

Market Explosion: Their products, now widely available in supermarkets, restaurants, and fast-food chains globally, have played a pivotal role in popularizing the plant-based diet beyond niche markets. Beyond Meat's success in mainstream retail and dining establishments has significantly contributed to the shift in consumer attitudes towards plant-based eating.

The Bigger Picture: Beyond Meat showcases the potential of innovation in addressing global sustainability and health concerns, proving that plant-based diets can be both environmentally beneficial and commercially viable. Their success story is a testament to the changing dynamics of consumer preferences, emphasizing the growing demand for sustainable and ethical food choices.

```
Pro Tip: When ideating, oscillate between the micro
and macro. Sometimes, personal challenges echo
universal sentiments.
```

Exercise Workshop: From Ideation to Opportunity Workshop

Cultivating Ideas:

- **Idea Generation Sprint:** Organize a structured brainstorming session focusing on a specific theme or problem area relevant to your industry. Encourage diversity in thought by including team members from various departments. Capture all ideas without judgment to foster creativity.
- **Trend Analysis Activity:** Assign a team to identify and analyze emerging trends within your target market. Utilize tools like Google Trends, industry reports, and social media to gather data. Present findings to the team and discuss how these trends can influence new product or service ideas.

Gap Identification and Validation:

- **Customer Pain Point Mapping:** Conduct a workshop aimed at identifying unmet needs within your target audience. Use customer interviews, surveys, or feedback from support channels to compile a list of common pain points. Map these against your current offerings to identify gaps.

- **Rapid Prototyping Session:** Select the most promising ideas from your brainstorming session and create simple prototypes or mockups. This could be as basic as sketches or more developed digital prototypes. Plan a validation strategy using A/B testing, customer interviews, or landing page conversions to gather feedback.

Iterative Development and Feedback Loop:

- **Feedback Integration Cycle:** Establish a recurring workshop where team members review customer feedback on existing products or services. Use this feedback to ideate improvements or iterations. Prioritize changes based on impact and feasibility.
- **Pivot Planning Meeting:** Should feedback indicate a significant shift in direction is needed, organize a pivot planning meeting. Discuss the implications of pivoting, outline a new strategic direction, and allocate resources accordingly.

Challenge For You: Identify a sector or niche within your industry that is currently underserved. Utilize the tools and strategies from this workshop to generate an innovative solution that addresses this gap. Compile your findings, ideas, and any initial feedback into a proposal for a new project or product line.

Are You Ready to Navigate from Ideation to Opportunity?
Transforming ideas into opportunities is an art that requires keen observation, relentless curiosity, and the courage to ven-

ture into uncharted territories. By engaging with the exercises outlined in this workshop, you're not just brainstorming; you're laying the groundwork for innovation that resonates deeply with your target market.

Coming Up Next: Chapter 4 delves into the art of crafting compelling value propositions. Discover how to articulate the unique benefits of your offerings, ensuring they resonate with your target audience and distinguish your venture in a crowded marketplace.

4

Crafting the Edge: Navigating Market Dynamics & Distinction

"Whenever you see a successful business,
someone once made a courageous decision."
— Peter Drucker

Embarking on the business odyssey is akin to setting sail on tumultuous seas. Here, mere comprehension is not enough; mastery is essential. The prowess of an entrepreneur isn't showcased merely in a product's brilliance but in understanding market whispers and crafting an unmistakable identity amidst the clamor. This chapter charts the course through the vast market oceans, deftly navigating the terrains of competition, and anchoring firmly with a resonant value proposition.

Opening Anecdote: The Story Behind LEGO's Reinvention

When sales plummeted in the early 2000s, LEGO faced a potential disaster. Instead of retreating, they decided to reinvent. Engaging with their loyal fan base, they introduced themed sets and even ventured into digital gaming and movies. Today, LEGO's story of reinvention is a testament to the power of innovation coupled with a deep understanding of one's core audience.

Mastering the Waves: Understanding the Market

- **The Market Telescope:** Observing before leaping is the entrepreneur's mantra. By segmenting markets, one zooms in, tailoring strategies to cater to nuanced niches with precision.
- **Crafting the Customer Blueprint:** The bedrock of business success lies in empathy and understanding. Delineating customer profiles enables crafting products that echo their desires and aspirations.
- **Gauging the Vastness:** An entrepreneur's compass is their understanding of market scale and potential. Recognizing its ebbs, flows, and expanses steers the venture with clarity.

Quick Thought:
Business is a nuanced symphony where attentive listening often trumps the loudest proclamations.

Attuning to the market's sotto voce can be the guiding beacon.

Competing Amidst the Currents: The Competitive Landscape

- **Spotting the Ships:** Identifying competitors, both direct and peripheral, sharpens the business acumen. By dissecting their strategies and trajectories, one gains invaluable insights and foresight.
- **Crafting the Unique Sail:** Every brand boasts its signature flair. This distinct identity, this competitive edge, is what sets ventures apart in a crowded marketplace.
- **The SWOT Compass:** The SWOT analysis serves as the North Star, enabling entrepreneurs to harness their strengths, mitigate weaknesses, and sidestep looming threats.

Etching the Mark: Value Proposition & Positioning

- **Crafting the Lighthouse:** Amidst the market haze, the value proposition emerges as a beacon. It attracts, assures, and accentuates a brand's unique essence to its audience.
- **Charting the Unique Course:** Effective positioning doesn't aim for mere distinction, but for indelibility. It etches a brand's identity firmly in the consumer psyche.
- **The Melody of the Brand:** A brand's narrative, its ethos, resonates as a melody. Crafting this melody to echo the brand's value, consistency, and uniqueness is paramount.

Entrepreneurship in Action: Key Ingredients

- **Strategic Market Insight**: Mastery over market dynamics begins with a strategic insight that combines observing market trends, understanding customer needs, and anticipating competitive moves. This deep market knowledge allows entrepreneurs to position their ventures for success in a crowded marketplace.
- **Distinctive Brand Identity**: Crafting a unique brand identity that resonates with your target audience is crucial. This involves not just visual elements, but also embedding your core values and mission into every aspect of your business, making your brand memorable and distinguishable from competitors.
- **Adaptive Positioning Strategy**: The ability to adapt and evolve your positioning strategy in response to market changes is a key ingredient for sustaining growth. This agility ensures that your venture remains relevant, appealing to both existing customers and attracting new ones by continuously offering value that meets their shifting expectations.

Case Study Highlight: Duolingo - Gamifying Language Learning

Innovative Genesis: Duolingo's journey began in a classroom at Carnegie Mellon University with Professor Luis von Ahn. Identifying the need for accessible language education, von Ahn envisioned a platform that could offer high-quality language learning to anyone, anywhere, for free.

Engagement Through Gamification: Duolingo introduced a revolutionary approach to language learning by incorporating gamification. This method transformed traditional learning experiences into engaging, bite-sized lessons that users could enjoy, making the daunting task of language learning fun and accessible.

Expanding Horizons: Duolingo's innovative platform quickly captured the hearts of learners worldwide, growing to hundreds of millions of users. Its success demonstrated the universal appeal of combining education with technology and entertainment.

Global Educational Impact: Today, Duolingo stands as a leader in online education, breaking down barriers to language learning and fostering global communication.

Duolingo exemplifies how innovative thinking and a focus on user engagement can disrupt traditional education models and create widespread impact.

```
Pro Tip: In business, prescience reigns supreme.
Adapting to change is commendable; anticipating and
pioneering it is transformative.
```

Exercise: Market Dynamics & Distinction Workshop

Market Mastery Exploration:

- **Market Mapping Exercise:** Choose a sector that interests you and map out the various market segments within it. For each segment, identify key characteristics, needs, and trends. This exercise aims to deepen your understanding of the market's complexity and where your potential venture could fit.

- **Customer Persona Development:** Create detailed customer personas for your chosen market segment. Focus on their demographics, psychographics, motivations, and pain points. Use this activity to refine your product or service concept to better meet these identified needs.

Competitive Strategy Formation:

- **Competitor Analysis Drill:** Select a market segment and list out potential competitors, including direct and indirect ones. Analyze their strengths, weaknesses, marketing strategies, and customer reviews. Use this analysis to identify gaps in the market that your business could fill.
- **Unique Value Proposition (UVP) Crafting:** Based on your competitor analysis, define your business's UVP. How does your product or service stand out? This should be a concise statement that clearly articulates why customers should choose you over the competition.

Brand Identity and Value Proposition Design:

- **Brand Story Workshop:** Develop your brand's story, focusing on its mission, vision, and the values that drive it. How does your brand relate to your target market on an emotional level? This narrative will form the core of your marketing and branding strategy.
- **Positioning Strategy Session:** Using the insights from your market mapping and customer persona development,

outline a positioning strategy for your venture. This should detail how you plan to position your brand in the minds of your target customers and differentiate it from competitors.

Challenge For You: Identify an industry trend that is currently shaping consumer behavior in your chosen market segment. Develop a mini-campaign or product feature that aligns with this trend, leveraging your unique value proposition to address it directly. Share your ideas in a team meeting or mentor session for feedback and further refinement.

Ready to Carve Your Niche? Understanding market dynamics and crafting a unique edge are foundational to making your mark in any industry. Through the exercises in this workshop, you're not just learning to navigate the competitive landscape; you're preparing to redefine it with your distinctive value proposition and brand identity.

Coming Up Next: Chapter 5 unveils the structural nuances of building a robust business model. Engage with key strategies that ensure your venture's stability, scalability, and sustainability, setting the stage for long-term success in the entrepreneurial journey.

5

Harnessing the Power of Business Model Innovation

"An entrepreneur paints success with brushes dipped in vision and strategy."
— Vanessa L. Weaver

In the bustling realm of startups, a powerful product or service is vital. However, even the most groundbreaking ideas may falter without a robust and innovative business model to support them. This chapter delves into the intricacies of business model innovation, offering strategies and insights to keep your venture at the forefront of industry evolution.

Opening Anecdote: Rethinking Glasses: The Zenni Optical Story

In the early 2000s, purchasing eyeglasses was often expensive and time-consuming. Zenni Optical transformed this experience by offering an online platform with affordable, stylish options. Their innovative direct-to-consumer model showcases the power of challenging industry norms.

> ### Quick Thought:
> *The entrepreneurial mindset isn't a bestowed legacy; it's a meticulously sculpted art. It isn't the eradication of fear but the audacity to march forward, undeterred by it.*

Entrepreneurship in Action: Key Ingredients

- **The Imperative of Business Model Innovation:** In a world of constant change, relying solely on product differentiation is a fleeting advantage. To ensure long-term viability and growth, startups must be willing to rethink and reinvent their business models.
- **Identifying Potential Shifts in the Market:** Understanding market dynamics is crucial. Shifts can arise from technological advancements, changes in customer preferences, or global economic shifts.
- **Adapting to the Digital Era:** The internet and digital technologies are not just tools; they can be the foundation of entirely new business models.

Case Study Highlight: Warby Parker - Disrupting the Eyewear Monopoly

Vision in a Classroom: At Wharton Business School, four friends identified a gap in the eyewear market. The industry's high markups and traditional business models were ripe for disruption.

Challenging the Giants with Affordability: Unlike the established eyewear giants that thrived on brand prestige, Warby Parker embarked on an affordability mission, prioritizing quality and design.

In-house Innovation: By designing in-house and cutting out middlemen, they offered designer glasses at a fraction of the cost, setting a new industry standard.

Connecting Directly with Customers: Their "Home Try-On" program, allowing customers to try on frames at home, added a personalized touch that resonated widely.

Beyond Glasses – Creating a Brand Movement: Their social impact initiative, "Buy a Pair, Give a Pair," highlighted their commitment to global vision health.

Tackling Challenges Head-On: Despite skepticism from traditional eyewear brands, Warby Parker's focus on customer experience, transparency, and impact solidified their market presence.

From Classroom Vision to Visionary Success: Today, Warby Parker stands as a beacon of how business model innovation can transform an industry, making eyewear accessible and fashionable.

Pro Tip: Embracing business model innovation isn't
about abandoning what works but enhancing and
evolving it to align with the changing landscape.

Exercise: Harnessing the Power of Business Model Innovation Workshop

Redefining the Blueprint:

- **Innovation Audits:** Embark on a comprehensive audit of your current business model. Identify areas ripe for innovation—be it your revenue streams, customer engagement strategies, or value delivery mechanisms. Reflect on how these components currently align with your market's needs and where there's room for transformation.
- **Market Shift Analysis:** Dedicate time to understanding recent shifts within your industry. Analyze emerging trends, technological advancements, and shifts in consumer behavior. How might these changes impact your business model? Utilize tools like PEST (Political, Economic, Social, Technological) analysis to structure your exploration.

Digital Transformation Dive:

- **Technology Integration Plan:** Assess your venture's digital maturity and identify key areas where technology can amplify your value proposition. Consider areas like customer experience, operational efficiency, or new product development. Plan steps to integrate relevant digital tools, platforms, or methodologies into your business model.

- **Digital Skillset Enhancement:** Organize a series of workshops or training sessions aimed at elevating your team's digital competencies. Cover topics critical to your business model innovation, such as data analytics, digital marketing, or software agility practices.

Customer-Centric Model Design:

- **Value Proposition Refinement:** Revisit and refine your value proposition with a fresh lens, especially considering the digital era's influence. How does digital transformation enable you to deliver unmatched value to your customers? Engage in customer feedback sessions to validate or pivot your proposition.
- **Customer Journey Mapping:** With your refined value proposition, map out the customer journey anew. Identify touchpoints that can be enhanced or newly created through digital means. Aim for a seamless, engaging customer experience that leverages digital tools to meet users' needs and exceed their expectations.

Strategic Innovation Implementation:

- **Business Model Prototyping:** Utilize the insights gathered from audits and analyses to prototype new business model variations. Approach this with a mindset of experimentation, ready to test, learn, and iterate.
- **Pilot and Feedback Loops:** Select one or two business

model innovations for pilot testing. Implement these on a small scale to gather real-time feedback and measure impact. Use these insights to adjust and refine before a full-scale rollout.

Challenge For You: Identify a disruptive technology trend relevant to your industry and brainstorm innovative ways it could be incorporated into your business model. Consider creating a small task force within your team to explore this over a month, culminating in a pitch session where you evaluate its feasibility and potential impact.

Through the lens of business model innovation, this chapter equips you with the strategies and mindset to not just navigate but redefine the competitive landscape. By staying adaptable, embracing digital transformation, and placing the customer at the core of your innovation efforts, your venture can achieve sustained growth and market leadership.

Coming Up Next: Chapter 6 delves into the critical importance of customer-centricity, exploring how placing the customer at the heart of your business strategy can revolutionize your growth trajectory and cement your competitive edge in the marketplace.

6

Building a Strong Startup Team

"Talent wins games, but teamwork and intelligence win championships."
- Michael Jordan

No entrepreneur can build a successful startup single-handedly. The strength of a startup often lies in the synergy of its team. This chapter navigates the intricate dynamics of building a formidable startup team, from harnessing top talent in a distributed workforce to fostering an inclusive and innovative team culture.

Opening Anecdote: Spotify - Unifying a Global Team:

In an era where many companies struggled with managing distributed teams, Spotify excelled. They decentralized decision-making, allowing autonomous teams, called "squads," to own their projects fully. Each squad, no matter where they were in the world, had a clear mission and the autonomy to achieve it. But autonomy did not mean isolation. Spotify invested in guild-coordinators who facilitated knowledge sharing across squads. They weren't just building a team; they were nurturing a global community. Their innovative team structure reflects the importance of both autonomy and unity in a distributed environment.

> **Quick Thought:**
> *Your startup's team isn't just a group of employees; it's the heart and soul of your venture. Like an orchestra, every individual plays a unique note, but together, they create a harmonious symphony.*

Attracting and Retaining Top Talent in a Distributed Workforce: In today's globalized and interconnected world, startups often operate with a distributed workforce. To attract and retain top talent in this distributed environment, startups must adopt specific strategies.

- **Building an Employer Brand:** Creating a compelling employer brand is crucial for attracting top talent. Startups need to define their company culture, values, and unique opportunities. Communicating these aspects effectively will help potential employees understand the exciting work environment and growth prospects within the startup.

- **Flexible Work Arrangements:** To attract and retain talent in a distributed workforce, offering flexible work arrangements is crucial. Startups should consider remote work options, flexible hours, and work-life balance initiatives. By providing flexibility, startups can accommodate the diverse needs of their employees and create a positive work environment.

- **Leveraging Technology for Collaboration:** Effective collaboration is key in a distributed workforce. Startups should leverage technology and tools that facilitate seamless communication, project management, and knowledge sharing among team members. Platforms for video conferencing, project management software, and virtual collaboration tools help bridge the distance and foster teamwork.

- **Emphasizing Personal and Professional Development:** Top talent is attracted to opportunities for growth and development. Startups should prioritize ongoing training, mentorship programs, and career advancement opportunities. By investing in the personal and professional development of their employees, startups create a culture of continuous learning and demonstrate their commitment to their team members' success.

Effective Team Building and Leadership Strategies: A great team is more than just a collection of individuals – it's a cohesive unit powered by vision, trust, and collaboration.

- **Defining Roles and Responsibilities:** Clearly defining roles and responsibilities helps avoid confusion and enhances team productivity. Startups should establish clear job descriptions, define individual and team goals, and foster a sense of ownership and accountability within the team. By establishing clear expectations, startups enable their team members to perform at their best.
- **Building a Complementary Team:** Creating a team with diverse skills and expertise is crucial for tackling the multifaceted challenges of a startup. Startups should identify the necessary skill sets, recruit team members with complementary strengths, and foster a collaborative environment where diverse perspectives are valued. By creating a team with diverse backgrounds, experiences, and skills, startups can enhance creativity, innovation, and problem-solving capabilities.
- **Effective Communication and Collaboration:** Open and effective communication is vital for team cohesion and productivity. Startups should establish transparent communication channels, promote active listening, and foster a culture of open feedback and constructive dialogue. Regular team meetings, virtual brainstorming sessions, and project updates help keep the team aligned, motivated, and engaged.
- **Empowering and Inspiring Leadership:** Effective leadership is essential for guiding and inspiring the team. Startups should empower their leaders to support and motivate team members. This involves providing guidance, support, and mentoring to help team members reach their full potential. By fostering a positive and inclusive work environment, startup leaders can create a culture

where team members feel valued, motivated, and inspired.
- **Connection:** Nurturing a culture of collaboration, diversity, and inclusion is another crucial aspect of building a strong startup team.

Nurturing a Culture of Collaboration, Diversity, and Inclusion: Diverse teams fuel innovation. But diversity without inclusion is mere tokenism. A strong team culture characterized by collaboration, diversity, and inclusion contributes to innovation and success.

- **Promoting Collaboration and Knowledge Sharing:** Creating an environment that values collaboration and knowledge sharing fosters creativity and innovation. Startups should encourage cross-functional collaboration, establish platforms for knowledge sharing (such as internal wikis or collaboration tools), and promote a culture of teamwork. Regular team meetings, brainstorming sessions, and collaborative projects can facilitate the exchange of ideas and perspectives, leading to more innovative solutions.
- **Embracing Diversity and Inclusion:** Diversity and inclusion are essential for building a strong and successful startup team. Startups should actively seek diversity in their hiring process, considering factors such as gender, ethnicity, age, background, and expertise. By embracing diversity, startups can tap into a wider range of perspectives, experiences, and ideas, which can lead to better problem-solving and decision-making. It is important to foster an inclusive work environment where everyone feels valued, respected, and empowered to contribute their

unique insights.

- **Training on Unconscious Bias and Cultural Sensitivity:** To foster an inclusive culture, startups should provide training on unconscious bias and cultural sensitivity to their team members. Unconscious biases can hinder collaboration and hinder the full potential of diverse teams. By raising awareness about these biases and promoting cultural sensitivity, startups can create a more inclusive and equitable work environment.
- **Establishing Employee Resource Groups:** Employee resource groups (ERGs) are voluntary, employee-led groups that provide support and promote the interests of specific communities within the organization. Startups can establish ERGs focused on various dimensions of diversity, such as gender, race, ethnicity, LGBTQ+, or disabilities. ERGs can foster a sense of belonging, provide networking opportunities, and contribute to a culture of inclusion.
- **Recognizing and Celebrating Achievements:** Acknowledging and celebrating the achievements of team members is important for building a positive and motivating work environment. Startups should recognize individual and team successes, whether through public recognition, rewards, or incentives. By appreciating and celebrating diverse contributions, startups reinforce the value of collaboration and create a culture where everyone feels motivated to excel.

Entrepreneurship in Action: Key Ingredients

1. **Visionary Leadership:** Leaders who understand the

dynamics of a distributed workforce and can guide teams while granting autonomy.

2. **Empowered Teams:** Squads had decision-making power and clear missions, fostering ownership and dedication.

3. **Strong Communication Channels:** Regular sync-ups, facilitated by guild coordinators, ensured knowledge sharing across teams.

Case Study Highlight: Atlassian: Diversity as a Strength

The Challenge: In a tech world dominated by large players and saturated with numerous tools catering to developers and project managers, Atlassian needed to distinguish its products and ethos. They had to ensure their products were not only functionally superior but also resonated with a broader, diverse audience.

The Strategy: Atlassian believed in the power of diverse teams to fuel innovation. They didn't merely pay lip service to the concepts of diversity and inclusion; they embedded them in their organizational DNA. By promoting Employee Resource Groups (ERGs) and actively seeking diversity in their hiring processes, they ensured a multitude of voices, backgrounds, and perspectives were involved in the product creation and enhancement processes.

The Transformation: Atlassian's flagship products, Jira and Confluence, are not just tools; they are a reflection of a diverse team's collective ingenuity. Their products are designed for accessibility, inclusivity, and ease of use, reflecting the varied inputs and insights from a global team.

The Impact: Atlassian's commitment to diversity and inclusion wasn't just a moral decision—it became a competitive advantage. Their products are used and loved by millions worldwide, and many users and clients often note how these tools seem "intuitively designed" for varied teams and needs. Behind this intuition lies the brilliance of a diverse team that brings its myriad experiences to the design table.

```
Pro Tip: Value commitment over association. When
building your team, seek individuals passionate
about the mission, not just the brand.
```

Exercise: Team Dynamics Mastery Workshop

Cultivating Leadership and Team Cohesion:

- **Leadership Style Assessment:** Conduct a self-assessment of your leadership style. Reflect on how your style influences team dynamics, motivation, and performance. Identify areas for improvement and commit to specific leadership development goals.
- **Team Cohesion Exercise:** Organize a workshop focused on strengthening team cohesion. Utilize team-building activities that emphasize trust, communication, and collaboration. Gather feedback from team members on the effectiveness of the exercise and their sense of belonging within the team.

Distributed Workforce Integration:

- **Remote Work Best Practices:** Develop a guide on best practices for remote work tailored to your startup's culture and operational needs. Include sections on communication protocols, digital tools for collaboration, and tips for maintaining work-life balance.
- **Virtual Team Building Event:** Plan and execute a virtual team-building event that caters to the interests and diversity of your team. Aim for activities that encourage interaction, laughter, and shared experiences, fostering a sense of unity despite physical distances.

Diversity and Inclusion Deep Dive:

- **Diversity Audit:** Perform a diversity audit of your startup. Evaluate your team composition, recruitment practices, and workplace policies through the lens of diversity and inclusion. Identify gaps and set actionable targets for improvement.
- **Inclusion Workshop:** Facilitate an inclusion workshop that educates your team on the importance of diversity, equity, and inclusion in the workplace. Cover topics such as unconscious bias, cultural competence, and creating an inclusive environment where every team member feels valued and heard.

Feedback Mechanisms and Continuous Improvement:

- **Feedback System Setup:** Establish or refine your startup's feedback mechanisms. This could involve setting up regular one-on-one meetings, anonymous feedback channels, or periodic surveys. Ensure there are clear processes for addressing and acting on feedback received.

- **Continuous Improvement Plan:** Create a continuous improvement plan for your team. Based on feedback and performance evaluations, identify key areas for development. Set goals for team training, knowledge sharing sessions, and cross-functional projects that drive collective growth and innovation.

Challenge For You: Identify one aspect of your startup team's dynamics that you believe could significantly benefit from enhancement—be it communication, diversity, or creative collaboration. Over the next month, implement targeted initiatives designed to address this area. Track progress through team feedback and performance metrics, adjusting your strategies as needed to achieve measurable improvement.

Fostering a high-performing startup team is a dynamic and ongoing process. Through the exercises outlined in this workshop, you're not only enhancing team cohesion and operational efficiency but also building a culture that attracts, nurtures, and retains top talent. As you progress, remember that the strength of your team directly influences the trajectory of your startup's success.

Coming Up Next: Chapter 7 is our first foray into Part Two **"Strategy Execution and Growth"** which delves into the intricacies of securing funding for your startup. Understand the when, why, and how of fundraising, exploring various avenues to fuel your venture's growth journey.

II

Part Two

Strategy Execution and Growth

7

Strategic Planning and Goal Setting

"Good fortune is what happens when opportunity meets with planning."
- Thomas Edison

S trategic planning and goal setting are not just buzzwords but the pivotal foundations of any successful startup. Serving as the compass for a startup's journey, they direct ventures from a mere idea to a tangible reality. This chapter unravels the essence of setting objectives, carving milestones, charting plans, and harnessing resources. When harmonized, these elements lead startups to their envisioned success.

Opening Anecdote: The Strategic Leap of Spanx by Sara Blakely

Before Spanx became a household name in women's shapewear, Sara Blakely was selling fax machines door-to-door in Florida. With $5,000 in savings and no formal business training, Blakely's journey to entrepreneurship was fueled by a singular product idea: footless pantyhose. Recognizing a gap in the market, she embarked on a mission not just to create a product but to revolutionize the industry. The road to Spanx's inception was paved with strategic decisions, from patenting the design herself to ensuring her product reached the shelves of high-end retail stores like Neiman Marcus. Blakely's clear vision and strategic planning propelled Spanx from a makeshift operation in her apartment to an iconic brand, making her the youngest self-made female billionaire. Her approach to goal setting, rooted in persistence and strategic outreach, exemplifies how visionary planning and precise execution can turn a simple idea into a global enterprise.

> **Quick Thought:**
> In the realm of startups, direction often overshadows speed. A meticulously charted plan ensures every step, regardless of its size, pushes the venture closer to its overarching vision.

Setting Clear Objectives: Clear objectives are paramount in strategic planning and goal setting. They bestow direction, clarity, and intent to the startup. Objectives need to be SMART—Specific, Measurable, Achievable, Relevant, and

Time-bound. For instance, Airbnb's early objective wasn't just to provide lodging but to "allow people to live like locals", a directive that vastly influenced their strategies.

Vision and Mission: A startup's vision and mission are the beacons guiding its course. The vision encapsulates the startup's long-haul aspirations, while the mission fleshes out the core actions driving this ambition. By carving out a resonant vision and mission, startups can align objectives seamlessly with their strategic roadmap. Case in point: Tesla's mission "to accelerate the world's transition to sustainable energy" clearly defines its focus and direction.

Long-Term Goals & Short-Term Objectives: While long-term goals outline a startup's aspirations spanning three to five years, short-term objectives condense these goals into immediate, actionable steps, typically spanning three to twelve months. They provide the momentum, ensuring continuous traction towards the final vision.

Defining Key Milestones: Milestones are the significant markers dotting a startup's growth timeline, providing opportunities for validation, reflection, and celebration.

- **Milestones as Progress Indicators**: They gauge a startup's progression. For instance, when Dropbox reached its first million users, it wasn't just a number but a validation of market acceptance.
- **Milestones for Validation and Learning**: They offer touchpoints for feedback and refinement. A tech startup, upon reaching its beta-testing milestone, might discover

critical UX issues, reshaping its product development trajectory.

Creating Actionable Plans and Timelines:

- **Breakdown of Tasks**: Dismantling objectives into tangible tasks helps in sequential planning. Defining actions, delegating responsibilities, and allocating timelines ensures a streamlined progression.
- **Sequencing and Dependencies**: Efficient sequencing avoids bottlenecks. For instance, a fintech startup can't test its payment gateway before ensuring security protocols are in place.
- **Resource Allocation**: Allocating resources, be it manpower, finances, or tech, is the backbone of execution. A classic example is how bootstrapped startups, with limited funds, prioritize critical growth areas to maximize ROI.

Agile and Iterative Approach: In the mercurial startup landscape, agility is paramount. Adopting an iterative approach ensures adaptability. A notable example is Instagram, which began as Burbn, a multi-featured app, but quickly pivoted focusing solely on photo-sharing upon recognizing its main appeal.

Entrepreneurship in Action: Key Ingredients

- **Defining Destination**: Grasp the 'where'. More than objectives, it's the ultimate goal and the roadmap to it.
- **Mapped Milestones**: Celebrate every win, however small. They validate, motivate, and recalibrate the journey.

- **Agile Approach**: In the ever-evolving business terrain, adaptability and iteration keep startups ahead of the curve.
- **Resource Realignment**: Recognize the finiteness of every asset and allocate strategically, continuously refining based on priorities.
- **Vision & Values Alignment**: Every decision should resonate with the startup's intrinsic values. It's the 'why' and 'how' that defines the journey.

Case Study Highlight: GreenLeaf Innovations - Revolutionizing Agri-tech for Small-Scale Farmers

Challenge and Pivot: In 2019, GreenLeaf Innovations found itself at a critical juncture. Despite developing advanced crop monitoring systems, they struggled to connect with their primary audience: small-scale farmers. The technology's complexity overshadowed its potential benefits, leading to a decline in sales and investor confidence. Recognizing this gap, GreenLeaf embarked on a mission to realign its offerings with the needs of its clientele, adopting the mantra, "Empowering Every Farmer with Tomorrow's Technology." This shift wasn't just about simplification; it was about making sophisticated technology accessible and practical for everyday use.

Strategic Overhaul: GreenLeaf's strategy pivoted from tech-centric to user-centric. They reimagined their products through the eyes of the farmers, focusing on usability and relevance. Short-term objectives were set to gather and implement user feedback, while long-term goals aimed at establishing GreenLeaf as a leader in the regional agri-tech landscape. This dual focus ensured immediate improvements in product design and user experience, setting the stage for broader market acceptance and expansion.

Triumphant Outcome: By 2021, GreenLeaf's strategic recalibration paid off. Sales surged by 250%, surpassing expectations and cementing the startup's place in the agritech market. Their systems, now praised for their user-friendly interface, gained popularity among a demographic traditionally wary of high-tech solutions. GreenLeaf's success extended beyond borders, as they expanded into neighboring countries, leveraging shared agricultural challenges to foster a wider community of users and advocates.

Lessons in Strategic Agility: GreenLeaf Innovations' journey from the brink of failure to market triumph underscores the power of strategic agility and market alignment. It highlights the importance of responsive innovation, where understanding and meeting customer needs is paramount. GreenLeaf's story serves as an inspiring example for startups in any sector: success lies in the ability to listen, adapt, and serve, transforming challenges into opportunities for growth and impact.

Pro Tip: Regularly revisit your strategic plan. In the dynamic startup environment, a periodic review ensures you're always aligned with your evolving goals and market conditions.

Exercise: Strategic Planning and Goal Setting Workshop

Defining Vision and Mission:

- **Vision and Mission Crafting Session:** Host a workshop with your team to refine or develop your startup's vision and mission statements. Use brainstorming techniques to capture the long-term aspirations (vision) and the daily operations and values that will get you there (mission). Ensure these statements are inspiring, clear, and directly aligned with the strategic direction of your startup.

SMART Goal Setting:

- **SMART Goals Workshop:** Break into small groups to identify and articulate specific short-term and long-term goals for your startup. Utilize the SMART framework to ensure each goal is Specific, Measurable, Achievable, Relevant, and Time-bound. Reconvene to discuss and refine these goals, ensuring they align with your overall strategic plan.

Milestone Mapping:

- **Key Milestone Identification Exercise:** Individually or in teams, list out the key milestones you anticipate for your startup over the next year. These should include product development benchmarks, customer acquisition targets, funding rounds, or any other significant achievements. Map these milestones on a timeline, discussing the dependencies and potential challenges associated with each.

Action Planning and Resource Allocation:

- **Action Plan Development:** Using the identified milestones as a guide, develop an action plan that breaks down the tasks required to achieve each milestone. Assign responsibilities and deadlines for each task, considering the sequencing and dependencies highlighted in your milestone mapping.
- **Resource Allocation Simulation:** Given a set scenario of limited resources (time, money, personnel), decide how you would distribute these resources among your planned activities. Discuss how these decisions align with your strategic priorities and what trade-offs might be necessary.

Adapting to Change:

- **Agility and Adaptation Workshop:** Engage in role-play or scenario planning exercises that simulate unexpected market changes or challenges. Practice adapting your strategies and goals in response, emphasizing the importance of agility and the ability to pivot as necessary for long-term success.

Reflection and Iteration:

- **Strategic Review Meetings:** Schedule regular strategic review meetings with your team to assess the progress towards your goals, discuss any adjustments needed in your action plans or resource allocations, and reaffirm your commitment to your startup's vision and mission.

Challenge For You: Over the next month, apply the strategic planning and goal-setting skills developed in this workshop to a specific project or aspect of your startup. Track progress against the SMART goals you've set, and hold a review session at the end of the month to evaluate achievements and learn from the outcomes.

By integrating strategic planning and goal setting into the fabric of your startup, you not only chart a course for success but also create a dynamic, responsive organization capable of navigating the complexities of the startup ecosystem.

Coming Up Next: Chapter 8 delves into the art of execution. Discover how to turn strategic plans and goals into actionable results, overcoming obstacles and driving your startup toward its ambitious objectives.

8

Product Development and Innovation

"Innovation distinguishes between a leader and a follower."
- Steve Jobs

The realm of startups thrives on innovation, not just in ideation but in execution. Here, a novel concept is only as good as its tangible implementation. This chapter delves into the intricate dance of transforming groundbreaking ideas into impactful products.

Opening Anecdote: The Dyson Vacuum Revolution

James Dyson grew frustrated with his vacuum's declining performance. Instead of settling, he embarked on a journey to reinvent the vacuum cleaner. After 5,127 prototypes, he launched a bagless vacuum utilizing cyclonic separation. Dyson's commitment to innovation transformed an everyday item into a superior product.

Understanding the MVP Concept: The Minimum Viable

Product (MVP) is akin to a prototype, a stripped-down version of a product containing just the essentials required to make it functional. The MVP serves a dual purpose: First, it allows startups to release a product rapidly to the market without investing significant resources. Second, it offers a direct channel to users, helping entrepreneurs gauge interest, collect data, and gather feedback. Think of the MVP as the foundational brick of your startup building, laying the groundwork upon which subsequent iterations and improvements will be made. It's the beginning of a feedback-driven, user-centric approach to product development.

Agile Methodologies: Agile is more than just a buzzword in the startup ecosystem; it's a mindset. It offers a set of principles and practices geared towards iterative development, where requirements and solutions evolve through a collaborative effort. By adopting agile, startups can be more responsive to changes, be it in the market, technology, or user feedback. Frameworks like Scrum and Kanban, which come under the agile umbrella, divide the development process into smaller, manageable chunks, allowing for periodic reviews, iterations, and improvements.

Quick Thought:

Innovation is not a solitary breakthrough but a continuous journey of iteration, feedback, and adaptation. The most enduring products are those that evolve through a relentless pursuit of perfection, always attuned to the shifting needs and desires of those they serve.

Feedback: The Cornerstone of Innovation: Feedback is the lifeblood of a startup's iterative cycle. Every piece of feedback, positive or negative, offers a lens into users' minds, helping startups understand their needs, preferences, and pain points. By actively seeking and valuing feedback, startups can ensure that their products are not developed in a vacuum but are firmly rooted in real-world requirements. Feedback prevents costly missteps, informs design and feature priorities, and fosters a relationship with users where they feel valued and heard.

Nurturing an Innovation Culture: Innovation isn't just about that lightbulb moment of a groundbreaking idea; it's a continuous process, a culture that permeates every layer of an organization. It's essential to foster a workplace environment where creativity is encouraged, failures are viewed as learning opportunities, and every team member feels empowered to contribute ideas. In such a nurturing environment, innovation thrives, leading to products that aren't just iterations of existing ones but are genuinely transformative. An innovative culture ensures that the startup remains adaptable, forward-looking, and always ready to ride the wave of the next big thing.

Entrepreneurship in Action: Key Ingredients

- **MVP Mastery:** Rapid learning, testing, and refinement lie at its heart.
- **Feedback Fluidity:** Let customer insights navigate the product's journey.
- **Cultural Creativity:** Innovation isn't a destination but a

journey, and the right environment can accelerate it.

Case Study Highlight: Raspberry Pi - Empowering Global Education Through Innovation

Origins of a Vision: Eben Upton and his team at the University of Cambridge noticed a distressing decline in the number of A-level students applying for computer science programs. This observation sparked a revolutionary idea: to create a low-cost, accessible computing platform that would inspire a new generation of learners. The Raspberry Pi, a compact and affordable computer, was conceived to reignite interest in computing among students, educators, and hobbyists worldwide.

Designing for Accessibility: From the beginning, Raspberry Pi was designed to be accessible. It was small enough to fit in a pocket and priced to fit a modest budget, breaking down barriers to technology education. Its open-source nature encouraged tinkering, modification, and learning, making it a versatile tool for users of all ages and skill levels.

A Catalyst for Learning: The Raspberry Pi Foundation's commitment went beyond the hardware. They provided educational resources, lesson plans, and community support to empower teachers and students. Their efforts have introduced millions to the possibilities of computing and programming, fostering a global community of creators and innovators.

Expanding Impact: Raspberry Pi's influence extends far beyond the classroom. It has become a staple in developing countries for its affordability and versatility, used in projects ranging from weather monitoring to wildlife conservation. The Raspberry Pi Foundation has also expanded its mission, advocating for digital making and creativity across the curriculum.

Legacy of Educational Innovation: Raspberry Pi's journey from an idea to a global educational movement underscores the transformative power of technology when aligned with a clear, altruistic mission. It exemplifies how innovation, driven by a desire to make a positive impact, can change the world.

The Raspberry Pi case study illustrates that with visionary thinking, commitment to accessibility, and a focus on community and education, startups can create products that not only succeed commercially but also contribute significantly to societal advancement.

```
Pro Tip: Innovation is as much about listening as it
is about creating. Keep customers at the core of the
development process for a product that's not just
novel but also deeply resonant.
```

Exercise: Product Innovation and Development Workshop

Understanding the MVP Concept:

- **MVP Design Sprint:** Organize a sprint to design the MVP for your product idea. Focus on identifying and incorporating only the essential features that solve your target customer's core problem. Conclude the sprint with a presentation of the MVP concept, inviting feedback from team members or stakeholders.

Implementing Agile Methodologies:

- **Agile Methodology Training:** Conduct a training session on Agile methodologies for your team, focusing on Scrum or Kanban. Use case studies or real projects to apply these frameworks, breaking down work into sprints or cycles, and emphasizing continuous improvement based on feedback.

Gathering and Utilizing Feedback:

- **Feedback Collection Workshop:** Create a workshop aimed at developing effective feedback collection strategies. Include designing surveys, setting up usability tests, and planning for A/B testing. Discuss how to prioritize feedback and integrate it into the product development process.

Nurturing an Innovation Culture:

- **Innovation Culture Day:** Dedicate a day to fostering innovation within your team. Include brainstorming sessions, encourage the sharing of wild ideas, and maybe even host a "hackathon" for small project prototypes. Highlight and reward innovative ideas that align with your product development goals.

Three Key Pillars of Product Development and Innovation Exercises:

- **MVP Mastery Activity:** Break into teams and outline the MVP for a hypothetical product based on a given customer problem. Each team pitches their MVP, focusing on rapid testing and learning cycles they would implement.
- **Feedback Fluidity Challenge:** Design a feedback loop for a current or upcoming product. Simulate a scenario where feedback drastically changes the product direction, and plan how to adapt your development process to this new feedback.
- **Cultural Creativity Workshop:** Facilitate a session on creating a sustainable innovation culture within your startup. Discuss barriers to innovation and develop strategies to overcome them, ensuring that creativity and innovation are not just encouraged but embedded in your startup's DNA.

Challenge For You: Identify a problem within your target market that hasn't been adequately addressed. Using the principles of MVP, Agile methodologies, and feedback integration, draft a preliminary plan for developing a product solution. Present your plan to a mentor or advisor and refine based on their insights.

In the ever-evolving landscape of startups, the ability to innovate and efficiently develop products is crucial. By engaging with these exercises, you're not just learning to navigate the complexities of product development; you're setting the stage for creating products that are truly innovative and capable of capturing the market.

Coming Up Next: Chapter 9 guides you through the essential strategies for positioning your innovative product in the market. Explore effective marketing and sales techniques to ensure your product not only reaches its target audience but also creates a lasting impact.

9

Crafting a Memorable Brand - The Soul of Your Startup

"Your brand is what other people say about you when you're not in the room."
— Jeff Bezos

B randing is more than just visual aesthetics. It's a strategic tool that communicates the essence of your startup, differentiates you in the marketplace, and resonates with your target audience.

Opening Anecdote: The Sweet Success of Ben & Jerry's

From a humble Vermont gas station to global ice cream fame, Ben Cohen and Jerry Greenfield's journey is about more than just ice cream. Their commitment to social justice, environmental causes, and community-centric values made them a beloved brand worldwide.

Building a Strong Brand Identity and Positioning

1. **Defining Brand Identity:** Your brand's essence is a melody, distinct and captivating, echoing your values, vision, and mission. The heart and soul of your brand come alive when these elements harmonize perfectly.
2. **Brand Positioning:** In the grand market orchestra, find your unique note. This distinct sound sets you apart and resonates with your audience.
3. **Consistent Brand Experience:** Every interaction should echo the same brand symphony, ensuring harmonious experiences across all touchpoints.

Developing a Marketing Plan

1. **Defining Marketing Objectives:** Just as a ship needs its North Star, your marketing endeavors need clear, guiding goals. Illuminate your path forward with precision and purpose.
2. **Target Market Analysis:** Navigate the vast seas of your target market, charting out the contours of customer aspirations, needs, and behaviors.
3. **Marketing Channels and Tactics:** In the vibrant marketplace bazaar, find your brand's best stall. Seek out those spaces where your stories resonate the loudest.
4. **Leveraging Digital Marketing Channels and Strategies:** Harness the winds of the digital realm to sail swiftly towards your audience, ensuring your brand stories are whispered across the vast digital landscapes.
5. **Human-Centric Branding:** Your tales should always echo the heartbeats of your audience. Let them be your

muse and inspiration.

> **Quick Thought:**
> *In the vibrant tapestry of the market, your brand is the thread that weaves through the consciousness of your audience, binding them with stories, values, and experiences that are uniquely yours. It's the silent yet eloquent ambassador of your vision, making every interaction not just a transaction but a moment of connection.*

Entrepreneurship in Action: Key Ingredients

- **Authentic Storytelling:** The core of a memorable brand lies in its authenticity. Craft stories that are true to your values and resonate with your audience, transforming customers into loyal advocates.
- **Strategic Consistency:** Ensure your brand's message and experience are consistently delivered across all channels. This uniformity strengthens brand recognition and fosters trust among your target audience.
- **Engagement and Adaptability:** Cultivate a brand that listens and adapts. Engage with your audience regularly to understand their evolving needs and preferences, allowing your brand to remain relevant and deeply connected to its community.

Case Study Highlight: Chobani - Revolutionizing the Yogurt Industry with Purpose

Founding Insights: Hamdi Ulukaya, spotting an opportunity in a discarded yogurt factory, embarked on a journey to introduce Greek yogurt to the American palate. His vision was clear: to craft a high-quality, nutritious product that caters to health-conscious consumers while embodying values of social responsibility.

Building a Brand on Goodness: Chobani's rise from a small startup to a market leader in the yogurt industry is a testament to the power of combining superior product quality with a strong ethical foundation. Ulukaya's commitment to using only natural ingredients and ensuring product accessibility played a pivotal role in building consumer trust and loyalty.

Community and Sustainability at Heart: From the outset, Chobani championed community enrichment and environmental sustainability. By offering substantial support to local farmers, fostering inclusivity in its hiring practices, and prioritizing eco-friendly production methods, Chobani not only set new industry standards but also cultivated a brand identity synonymous with goodness and generosity.

Innovating for Impact: Chobani's initiatives, such as the Chobani Incubator for food entrepreneurs, reflect its dedication to nurturing innovation and driving positive change within the broader food industry. These efforts underscore the brand's commitment to supporting emerging businesses that share its vision for a healthier, more sustainable world.

A Legacy of Leadership: Chobani's journey illuminates the path for startups aiming to merge profitability with purpose.

Ulukaya's leadership underscores the significance of building a brand that stands for more than just its products, demonstrating that genuine commitment to social and environmental causes can propel a company to unprecedented success.

Chobani's story exemplifies how startups can achieve remarkable growth by embedding purpose into their brand DNA. It illustrates the enduring impact of ethical leadership and the transformative potential of aligning business practices with broader societal values.

```
Pro Tip: A strong brand transcends products or
services; it builds emotional connections.
```

Exercise: Brand Essence Workshop

Crafting Your Brand's Core:

1. **Brand Storytelling Session:** Gather your team for a storytelling workshop. Reflect on your startup's journey, values, and vision. Craft a compelling brand story that encapsulates the essence of your startup. Consider how your unique story differentiates you in the market.
2. **Vision and Values Alignment:** Develop a vision and values statement for your startup. Utilize insights from your brand storytelling session to ensure alignment. This statement will guide your branding and operational decisions, ensuring consistency across all touchpoints.

Positioning Your Brand:

1. **Unique Value Proposition Development:** Identify what sets your startup apart. Host a brainstorming session focused on your startup's unique value proposition (UVP). How does your product or service solve problems differently? Craft a clear, concise UVP that will be central to your marketing and brand communication.
2. **Competitive Landscape Analysis:** Conduct a workshop to analyze your competitors and their positioning. Identify gaps in the market that your startup can uniquely fill. Use this analysis to refine your brand positioning, ensuring it resonates with your target audience and distinguishes you from competitors.

Building a Consistent Brand Experience:

1. **Customer Journey Mapping:** Map out the customer journey, from awareness to loyalty. Identify key touchpoints and ensure that your brand messaging is consistent and impactful at each stage. This exercise will help you understand where you can enhance the brand experience to better meet customer needs.
2. **Brand Guidelines Development:** Create comprehensive brand guidelines that encompass visual identity, tone of voice, and overall brand ethos. These guidelines will ensure consistency across all marketing materials, customer interactions, and product development.

Developing a Strategic Marketing Plan:

1. **SMART Marketing Objectives Setting:** Define specific, measurable, achievable, relevant, and time-bound (SMART) marketing objectives. These should align with your overall business goals and brand strategy.
2. **Channel Strategy Workshop:** Evaluate various marketing channels for their effectiveness in reaching your target audience. Develop a multi-channel strategy that leverages both digital and traditional marketing to tell your brand's story and engage with customers.

Leveraging Digital Marketing for Brand Growth:

1. **Digital Marketing Exploration:** Dive into the digital marketing landscape to identify trends and tools that can amplify your brand's reach and engagement. Consider SEO, content marketing, social media, and email marketing as potential pillars of your digital strategy.
2. **Content Creation Marathon:** Organize a content creation sprint with your team. Focus on generating a variety of content (blog posts, social media updates, videos) that reflects your brand identity and can be used across different digital platforms.

Fostering Human-Centric Branding:

1. **Community Engagement Plan:** Design a plan to actively engage with your community both online and offline. Consider hosting events, creating a brand ambassador program, or partnering with like-minded organizations to deepen connections with your audience.
2. **Feedback Loop Integration:** Establish a system for

collecting and acting on customer feedback. Use this feedback to continuously refine your brand and product offerings, ensuring they remain aligned with customer needs and expectations.

Challenge for You: Take a step back and critically assess your brand through the eyes of a customer. Identify three areas where your brand's identity, message, or experience could be enhanced. Implement one change based on this assessment and monitor the impact over the next month.

By engaging with these exercises, you're not just building a brand; you're cultivating a living entity that grows, evolves, and resonates deeply with your audience.

Coming Up Next: Next, we'll explore the dynamic world of growth hacking, equipping you with the tools to not only capture attention but to sustain and grow your startup's impact.

10

Sales and Customer Acquisition - Crafting a Growth Blueprint

"In every sale, there's a tale – of trust, of need, of connection."
— Javier O. Ruiz

Sales and customer acquisition are the heartbeats of startups, echoing the dreams of founders and the needs of customers. In this chapter, we'll walk through the corridors of sales strategies, cross bridges built on customer relationships, and set our sights on the horizon of sustainable growth.

Opening Anecdote: The Dominance of Zoom in a Pandemic World

When face-to-face meetings became a health risk, Zoom became a household name overnight. Eric Yuan's commitment to a reliable, user-friendly platform made global connectivity during a pandemic not only possible but also efficient.

Crafting Effective Sales Strategies and Techniques

- **Understanding the Sales Process**: The sales journey, like any great adventure, has its path. From the first whisper of a potential lead to the victorious chorus of a closed deal, it's a narrative that needs flow and finesse. Action Steps: Script your sales tale, hold regular team gatherings around the storytelling fire, and adapt based on the tales from the field.
- **Target Customer Profiles**: To tell a compelling story, know your audience. Dive into their world, understand their desires, and craft tales that resonate. Action Steps: Venture into the land of market research, sculpt detailed customer personas, and weave product features into their narratives.
- **Articulating a Value Proposition**: Your story's essence is what sets it apart. Whisper it, shout it, but ensure your audience feels its uniqueness. Action Steps: Gather your team for tale-spinning sessions, seek feedback from your audience, and echo a consistent theme across every chapter.
- **Developing Sales Techniques**: The magic lies not just in the tale but in the telling. Let every sale be a heartfelt

narration, an answer to a need, a bond formed. Action Steps: Host storytelling masterclasses, simulate customer engagements, and arm your narrators with techniques to enchant.

Building Customer Relationships and Effective Sales Funnels

1. **Nurturing Customer Relationships**: Beyond the tale's climax is the sequel – the enduring bond forged with your audience. Action Steps: Design post-tale engagements, listen to your readers, and address their musings promptly.
2. **Sales Funnel Creation**: Every chapter of the customer's journey, from curiosity to commitment, is a part of your epic. Action Steps: Ponder over their footsteps, pinpoint moments of hesitation, and smooth their path forward.

> *Quick Thought:*
>
> *The art of selling is not in the transaction, but in creating connections that resonate. It's about understanding deep needs and offering solutions that matter. In every successful sale, there lies a story of empathy, insight, and a bridge built between need and fulfillment.*

Leveraging Marketing Automation for Enhanced Outreach

Why Automation Matters: Let your tales spread far and

wide, whispered by the winds of automation, ensuring every listener feels the personal touch. Action Steps: Seek the scrolls of automation wisdom, blend them into your sales narrative, and let them evolve with changing times.

Measuring and Optimizing Sales Performance for Sustainable Growth

1. **Tracking Sales Metrics**: In the tapestry of numbers, patterns emerge, tales of triumph and lessons of yore. Action Steps: Employ the oracles of analytics, gather around for monthly tale reviews, and carve benchmarks for the epics ahead.

2. **Investing in Sales Analytics**: With data as your compass, navigate the ever-shifting sands of the market. Action Steps: Dedicate treasures to advanced analytics, mentor your team in its arts, and adapt your strategies to the songs of the data.

3. **Sales Process Refinement**: Just as tales evolve with each retelling, so must your sales saga with the changing winds of the market. Action Steps: Convene at the strategy roundtable each season, collate wisdom from all quarters, and amend your story as needed.

Entrepreneurship in Action: Key Ingredients

- **Empathetic Engagement:** Understanding the heartbeats of your customers, feeling their needs as your own, and responding with solutions that truly matter.
- **Strategic Storytelling:** Weaving your product's unique value into compelling narratives that captivate and con-

vince.

- **Dynamic Adaptation:** Being agile in your approach, ready to evolve your sales strategies in response to market feedback and technological advancements.

Case Study Highlight: HubSpot's Revolution in Sales and Marketing

Founding Vision: HubSpot was founded by Brian Halligan and Dharmesh Shah out of a shared realization that traditional marketing techniques were becoming less effective in a digital world. They envisioned a platform that would help businesses attract, engage, and delight customers in a more organic and meaningful way.

Inbound Marketing Pioneer: HubSpot became synonymous with inbound marketing, a strategy focused on creating valuable content and experiences tailored to customers. Unlike outbound marketing's disruptive techniques, HubSpot's approach aimed to draw customers through the relevance and helpfulness of content, fundamentally changing how companies interact with their audiences.

Expansion and Integration: As HubSpot grew, it didn't just stick to marketing tools. It expanded into sales and service sectors, offering an integrated suite to manage customer relationships comprehensively. This holistic approach helped businesses streamline operations, ensuring consistent and personalized customer interactions across all touchpoints.

Educational Approach to Growth: Key to HubSpot's strategy was its investment in educational content and certification programs. By providing extensive resources on inbound marketing, sales strategies, and customer service best practices, HubSpot positioned itself as an authority in the field, fostering a community of informed users and advocates.

Sustainable Growth: HubSpot's growth has been marked by a commitment to ethical sales practices and customer-centric growth strategies. Its success demonstrates how aligning sales and marketing efforts with customer needs leads to sustainable business growth. Today, HubSpot stands as a testament to the power of inbound marketing and the importance of building a sales strategy that prioritizes long-term relationships over short-term gains.

HubSpot's journey from a simple idea to a global leader in inbound marketing underscores the importance of innovation, customer focus, and ethical practices in sales and customer acquisition. Their legacy is a blueprint for startups aiming to navigate the competitive landscape of digital marketing and sales with integrity and effectiveness.

```
Pro Tip: Nurture the storytellers of your realm —
your sales team. For their tales, spun with skill
and heart, can change the fate of kingdoms.
```

Exercise: Sales and Customer Acquisition Mastery Workshop

Crafting Your Sales Narrative:

- **Narrative Development Activity:** Reflect on your startup's core value proposition. Craft three distinct sales narratives, each tailored to different customer personas. Role-play these narratives within your team or with a small focus group to identify which resonates the most and why.

Deep Dive into Customer Personas:

- **Persona Workshop:** Build detailed customer personas that include demographics, psychographics, pain points, and aspirations. Use these personas to create tailored sales strategies, customizing your approach to meet each persona's unique needs.

Sales Funnel Optimization:

- **Funnel Analysis Task:** Map out your existing sales funnel from awareness to conversion. Identify at least two areas where prospects drop off or engagement wanes. Develop strategies to address these gaps and improve conversion rates.

Feedback Integration for Improvement:

- **Feedback Collection Initiative:** Design a system to

collect and analyze feedback from every stage of the customer journey. Use this feedback to host a workshop aimed at refining your sales process, ensuring it meets customer needs more effectively.

Leveraging Technology for Sales Efficiency:

- **Technology Utilization Plan:** Evaluate and integrate sales automation tools that enhance efficiency and personalization. Plan a training session for your team on using these tools to maximize outreach and engagement.

Performance Tracking and Analytics:

- **Analytics Workshop:** Gather sales data and conduct a comprehensive analysis with your team. Identify trends, assess performance against KPIs, and set actionable goals for improvement. Incorporate a regular review cycle to continuously refine your sales strategies.

Innovative Sales Tactics Exploration:

- **Innovation Brainstorming Session:** Organize a brainstorming session to explore innovative sales tactics. Consider new technologies, unconventional engagement platforms, and creative partnership opportunities. Select one or two ideas for pilot testing.

Challenge For You: Over the next two weeks, embark on a journey of profound listening. Engage with your customers, not just as buyers but as the voices that guide the evolution of your startup. Pay close attention to their stories, needs, and feedback. Let this insight be the north star for refining your sales approach, enhancing your value proposition, and deepening your customer connections. Set specific objectives to implement based on what you learn, and monitor the impact these adjustments have on your sales outcomes and customer satisfaction.

Are You Ready to Transform Your Sales and Customer Acquisition Strategy? Excelling in sales and customer acquisition transcends mere tactics and transactions. It's about building relationships, understanding deep-seated needs, and delivering value that resonates on a personal level. Through the exercises presented, you're not merely aiming to increase numbers but to forge a growth pathway that is sustainable, impactful, and deeply connected to your customers' journeys. This approach sets a solid foundation for not just surviving but thriving in the competitive startup ecosystem.

Onward to Financial Mastery: As we turn the page, Chapter 11 beckons us into the critical realm of financial management and scalability. Here, we will uncover the financial strategies that ensure your startup's growth is not only rapid but also resilient and sustainable. Prepare to dive deep into budgeting, fundraising, and financial planning—essential skills for any entrepreneur ready to take their startup to new heights. Join us as we navigate these financial waters, laying the groundwork for a future where your startup not only succeeds but excels.

11

Scalability and Growth Strategies

"Success is the sum of small efforts, repeated day in and day out."
— Robert Collier

G rowth is a goal, but scalability is the method. Every startup has aspirations of expanding, but the strategies applied determine the quality and sustainability of that growth. Dive into this chapter as we unravel the essentials of scaling operations, widening market horizons, and forging partnerships that can exponentially increase your reach and impact.

Opening Anecdote: How Etsy Crafted its Niche

In a world dominated by retail giants, Etsy carved its niche by offering a platform for artisans to sell unique, handcrafted goods. Their commitment to supporting small businesses and emphasizing sustainability set them apart in the e-commerce world.

Strategies for Scaling Operations and Managing Growth

- **Establishing Scalable Systems and Processes:** As your startup sails the vast sea of growth, ensure it's powered by agile, scalable systems that adjust to the winds of change. Streamlined, technology-driven systems are paramount to maintain quality as you venture forth.
- **Building a High-Performing Team:** Growth is as much about numbers as it is about people. It's a symphony where every role counts. Ensure that your orchestra – your team – is both talented and adaptable to the evolving tunes of business. Talent is your biggest asset.
- **Managing Financial Resources:** Every entrepreneurial saga has a treasury tale. Guard it. Nurture it. Your startup's fiscal fitness is the backbone of its growth story. Your startup's financial health often determines its growth capacity.

Expanding into New Markets and Customer Segments

- **Market Research and Analysis:** Every new land holds secrets. Decipher them. Ensure you comprehend the nuances and melodies of the new market you seek to serenade. Understanding the new market terrain is essential.
- **Tailoring Value Propositions:** Every audience has its unique rhythm. Dance to it. Mold your offerings, so they echo in the hearts of your new clientele. Every market has unique needs. Adapt your offerings to resonate.
- **Localization and Cultural Adaptation:** Embrace the local folklore. Your brand should become a cherished

chapter in the local tapestry. Respect and integrate local traditions and customs.

Leveraging Partnerships and Strategic Alliances

- **Identifying Strategic Partners:** In the dance of business growth, finding the right partner can turn a waltz into a gala. Sync your steps with entities that resonate with your entrepreneurial tune. Collaborate with entities that complement your business. Shared visions and resources can create mutual growth opportunities.
- **Building Strong Relationships:** Behind every corporate handshake lies a bond of trust and shared dreams. Nurture it. Let your alliances be built on trust, mutual respect, and shared visions. Trust and dialogue are essential. Ensure regular check-ins, transparency, and shared goals.
- **Joint Marketing and Co-branding:** Two voices, singing in harmony, can be more enchanting than a solo. Let collaborative campaigns be the duet that captivates the market. Collaborative campaigns can significantly amplify your market presence.

Quick Thought:

Scalability is not merely about enlarging the footprint of your startup but about doing so with precision and foresight. It's about ensuring that each step towards growth is sustainable, impactful, and aligned with the core mission of your business.

Entrepreneurship in Action: Key Ingredients

- Streamline and automate processes.
- Invest in employee development and culture-building.
- Monitor financial health and adapt strategies accordingly.
- Thoroughly research new markets before expansion.
- Seek synergistic partnerships that align with your vision.

Case Study Highlight: Zoom's Meteoric Rise in Digital Communication

Innovative Beginnings: Founded by Eric Yuan, Zoom was born out of a desire to make remote communication seamless and reliable, despite the crowded market of video conferencing tools. With a focus on user-friendly features and superior performance, Zoom set itself apart from the outset.

Rapid Expansion: As the COVID-19 pandemic unfolded, Zoom's daily meeting participants skyrocketed from 10 million to over 300 million in just a few months, testing the company's scalability and infrastructure. This unprecedented growth highlighted Zoom's effective scalability strategies and its infrastructure's capability to handle sudden surges in demand.

Addressing Challenges Head-On: Amidst its rapid growth, Zoom faced significant security and privacy concerns. Eric Yuan's proactive and transparent approach to addressing these issues—implementing end-to-end encryption and enhancing security features—demonstrated a commitment to ethical growth and user trust.

A Model for Scalable Growth: Today, Zoom is not just a tool for corporate meetings but a platform that connects people across various sectors globally. Its journey from a startup to a key player in digital communication showcases the importance of innovation, ethical practices, and the ability to scale effectively in response to dynamic market demands.

Zoom's story is a testament to the power of visionary leadership and scalable, sustainable growth strategies in building a business that not only leads the market but also changes the way the world communicates.

Pro Tip: Scalability is not just about expansion, but doing so efficiently. Always weigh the benefits against the operational and financial costs.

Exercise: Growth and Scalability Action Plan Workshop

Operational Efficiency Improvement:

- **Process Mapping Exercise:** Identify and map out all critical operational processes within your startup. For each process, mark its current efficiency on a scale of 1-10 and list potential areas for automation or streamlining.
- **Bottleneck Analysis:** Focus on processes rated below 5. Conduct a root cause analysis to understand the bottlenecks. Brainstorm solutions with your team, aiming for quick wins that can improve efficiency.

Market Expansion Analysis:

- **Emerging Market Exploration:** Select two potential markets for expansion. Use a mix of market research, customer interviews, and competitive analysis to gather insights. Create a comprehensive report on each, focusing on market size, customer needs, and competitive landscape.
- **Value Proposition Adaptation:** Based on your market research, adapt your startup's value proposition for each new market. Draft a message matrix that outlines how your core product benefits align with the identified customer needs and cultural nuances.

Strategic Partnership Development:

- **Potential Partner Mapping:** Create a list of potential strategic partners in both your current and target markets. Evaluate each based on strategic fit, market reach, and potential for collaborative innovation.
- **Partnership Outreach Plan:** For the top three potential partners identified, develop a customized outreach plan. This should include a clear proposition of mutual benefits, ideas for collaborative projects, and proposed terms for a partnership agreement.

Scalability Self-Assessment:

- **Scalability Readiness Checklist:** Develop a checklist that covers key areas critical to scalability, including technology infrastructure, team capacity, financial resources, and customer support. Rate your startup's readiness in each area and identify gaps.

- **Actionable Roadmap:** For each gap identified in the scalability readiness checklist, outline specific actions needed to address them. Assign responsibilities and set deadlines for each action item to ensure accountability.

Reflection and Future Planning:

- **Growth Reflection Journal:** Maintain a journal over the next month, documenting your thoughts and observations as you implement aspects of your scalability plan. Note any unexpected challenges, opportunities that arose, and how your strategy evolved in response.
- **Scalability Vision Board:** Create a vision board that represents your startup's future growth and scalability. Include images, quotes, and symbols that inspire and align with your scalability goals. Place it in a visible area to remind you and your team of the growth journey ahead.

Challenge For You: Reflect on your startup's journey towards scalability. Identify one aspect that poses the most significant challenge to scalable growth. Is it operational efficiency, market expansion, or forging the right partnerships? Devise a targeted strategy to tackle this challenge over the next quarter. Document your approach, implement it, and monitor the outcomes. Share your insights and progress with your team or within your entrepreneurial network to foster a culture of continuous improvement and strategic growth.

Are You Prepared to Scale Your Vision? Embarking on a scalability and growth journey requires more than ambition; it demands a blueprint that marries innovation with efficiency, expansion with insight, and partnerships with synergy. Through the exercises and strategies outlined, you're not just aiming for growth; you're sculpting a scalable enterprise poised for enduring success.

Next Steps on Your Entrepreneurial Quest: As we close this chapter on scalability and growth strategies, we pave the way for the next frontier - "Financial Management and Fundraising." Dive deep into the financial strategies that fortify your startup's foundation, ensuring it not only grows but thrives financially. Prepare to navigate the complexities of fundraising, budget management, and financial forecasting, equipping your startup with the acumen to secure its future.

12

Financial Management and Funding

"Finance is not merely about making money. It's about achieving our deep goals and protecting the fruits of our labor."
– Robert J. Shiller

Money is the lifeblood of every startup. Without a solid grip on finances, even the most ground-breaking idea can wither away. This chapter breaks down the financial maze, helping you strategize for success.

Opening Anecdote: Amazon's Growth Trajectory

From selling books in Jeff Bezos' garage to becoming a global e-commerce titan, Amazon's journey is a masterclass in scaling a startup. Their continuous reinvestment strategy and commitment to customer-centricity propelled them to unparalleled heights.

Laying the Foundation: Financial Planning and Forecasting

- **Setting Financial Goals and Objectives:** In the grand opera of business, financial goals set the rhythm, orchestrating harmony between dreams and practicalities. Goals drive focus. Align them with your broader business objectives.
- **Creating Financial Projections:** Gazing into the fiscal crystal ball, entrepreneurs anticipate the turns and tunnels, paving the path to progress. Predict your startup's fiscal future by analyzing key data points.
- **Conducting Sensitivity Analysis:** In the realm of finance, the only certainty is uncertainty. Be prepared, be adaptable, and let resilience be your mantra. How resilient are your financial plans to changes? Assess and iterate.

Fueling the Engine: Understanding Funding Options

- **Bootstrapping:** There's profound merit in self-sufficiency. Sometimes, the initial wind beneath a startup's wings is the founder's own conviction and resources. Sometimes, the best investment comes from your pocket.
- **Angel Investors and Venture Capital:** In this dance of dreams and capital, finding the right partner can elevate your venture to dizzying heights. Exchange equity for capital and expertise.
- **Crowdfunding:** Let your story resonate, and watch a symphony of supporters rally behind your vision. Let the crowd be your investor.
- **Grants and Government Funding:** Sometimes, the

winds of societal good and governmental backing can propel your startup forward without diluting ownership. Tap into funds without relinquishing equity.

Keeping the Lights On: Managing Cash Flow

- **Implementing Cash Flow Forecasting:** In the ebb and flow of cash, foresight is the lighthouse, preventing ventures from running aground. Predicting your financial ebbs and flows can be a lifesaver.
- **Optimizing Accounts Receivable and Payable:** A game of balances, where timeliness ensures the financial scales remain tipped in favor of growth. Your cash flow's health is often dictated by when you pay and get paid.
- **Controlling Expenses:** Every expense tells a tale. Ensure yours is one of judicious choices, propelling your startup's narrative towards greater fiscal health. Every penny saved can be a penny reinvested.

Quick Thought:

Effective financial management and funding are about more than numbers; they embody the strategic foresight and stewardship guiding a startup towards long-term sustainability and success.

Entrepreneurship in Action: Key Ingredients

- **Strategic Financial Planning:** Aligning financial goals with business objectives to navigate growth sustainably.

- **Adaptive Funding Strategies:** Exploring and utilizing diverse funding sources to fuel expansion while maintaining operational integrity.
- **Proactive Cash Flow Management:** Ensuring liquidity and financial health through meticulous cash flow forecasting and management.

Case Study Highlight: Palantir's Financial Strategy: Harnessing Data for Stability

Origin and Evolution: Founded with a vision to transform how organizations analyze information, Palantir Technologies quickly became pivotal in intelligence and defense sectors with its advanced data analytics capabilities. Yet, as the company ventured into commercial markets, it encountered the unpredictable nature of financial management in the tech startup landscape.

Challenge: Palantir faced the daunting task of managing volatile sales cycles and diversifying revenue streams, crucial for sustaining growth and ensuring stable cash flow. The variability in project timelines and client payments posed significant risks to operational efficiency and financial health.

Innovative Solution: Leveraging its expertise in data analysis, Palantir applied its own technologies to internal financial processes. They developed a sophisticated system to dissect and comprehend complex financial data, enabling real-time analytics for forecasting and resource allocation.

Action Steps:

- **Data-Driven Financial Forecasting:** Palantir implemented predictive analytics to anticipate financial trends, assess risks, and identify opportunities, ensuring strategic decision-making was grounded in comprehensive data insights.

- **Optimizing Financial Operations:** Through the analysis of accounts receivable and payable, Palantir optimized cash flow management, reducing the impact of sales cycle volatility and improving liquidity.
- **Strategic Resource Allocation:** By employing their analytics platform, Palantir could allocate resources more efficiently, prioritizing investments in projects with the highest potential return or strategic value.

Outcome: This approach transformed Palantir's financial management, turning potential vulnerabilities into strengths. The company achieved greater stability in cash flow, enhanced operational efficiency, and a more strategic approach to financial planning and resource management.

Broader Impact: Beyond its own financial health, Palantir's approach demonstrated the power of leveraging core technological competencies to address business administration challenges. This strategy not only solidified Palantir's standing in its primary sectors but also positioned the company as a leader in demonstrating the value of data-driven financial management in the tech industry.

Legacy of Innovation: Palantir's journey highlights the critical role of innovative financial management strategies in the growth and sustainability of tech startups. By integrating its data analytics prowess with financial processes, Palantir set a benchmark for how startups can harness technology to navigate financial complexities, ensuring agility and resilience in the face of uncertainty.

This case study exemplifies the symbiotic relationship between product innovation and financial strategy, illustrating that the technologies developed to serve clients can also empower startups to achieve financial stability and operational excellence. Palantir's experience serves as an inspiration for startups navigating the intricate financial landscapes, showcasing the indispensable value of data in crafting a robust financial management framework.

```
Pro Tip: In the world of startups, cash flow is
king. Regular financial health check-ups can be the
difference between thriving and just surviving.
```

Exercise: Financial Mastery Workshop

Financial Goals Mapping:

- **Goal-Setting Exercise:** Identify financial milestones for the next 1, 3, and 5 years. These should include revenue targets, profitability goals, and other financial KPIs important to your startup's success. Create a visual map of these goals to keep them in focus.
- **Alignment Check:** Ensure these financial goals align with your overall business strategy and mission. Discuss with your team how each department can contribute to achieving these goals.

Cash Flow Analysis:

- **Cash Flow Forecasting Activity:** Utilize a template to project your startup's cash flow for the next 12 months. Include expected income, expenses, and how you plan to address any cash shortfalls or surpluses.
- **Sensitivity Analysis:** Adjust your forecast based on best-case and worst-case scenarios, analyzing how changes in market conditions, sales forecasts, or expenses could impact your cash flow.

Funding Strategy Plan:

- **Exploration Task:** Research and list at least three potential funding sources that fit your startup's current stage and future growth plans. These could include angel investment, venture capital, grants, or crowdfunding.
- **Pros and Cons Analysis:** For each funding source, evaluate the advantages and disadvantages, considering factors like dilution of equity, repayment terms, and alignment with your startup's values and goals.

Expense Management Challenge:

- **Expense Audit:** Conduct a thorough review of your startup's expenses over the last quarter. Categorize each expense and identify areas where costs can be reduced or eliminated without impacting product quality or growth.
- **Budget Optimization Plan:** Develop a plan to optimize your budget, reallocating savings to higher ROI activities or to bolster your cash reserves.

Challenge For You: Over the next month, implement the "Expense Management Challenge" from the Financial Mastery Workshop. Document the process, including any changes made and the impact on your startup's financial health. Share the outcomes and lessons learned with your team, fostering a culture of financial mindfulness.

Navigating Financial Waters: Mastering financial management and funding is pivotal for steering your startup through the tumultuous waters of growth and competition. The exercises outlined above are designed to enhance your financial acumen, preparing you for the challenges and opportunities that lie ahead.

Next Steps: As you turn the page to the next chapter of your entrepreneurial journey, remember that financial savvy is not just about survival—it's about thriving. Embrace the principles of financial management and funding to build a resilient, scalable startup poised for enduring success.

III

Part Three

Leadership and Management in a Distributed Workforce

13

Leading Distributed Teams

*"To lead a distributed team, one must be both a
technology champion and a human-centric guide."*
— Fernando Dal Re

I n a world that's seamlessly connected yet physically
dispersed, leading distributed teams has become the new
norm. This chapter delves into strategies, tools, and
techniques to ensure your leadership is as effective remotely
as it is face-to-face.

Opening Anecdote: The Success Secrets of Basecamp

As one of the pioneers in project management software,
Basecamp's commitment to simplicity and effective remote
work practices set them apart. Their transparency about work-
from-home strategies has been an inspiration for companies
worldwide.

Foundation Strategies for Remote Leadership

- **Leveraging Digital Communication:** In the vast expanse of digital workspaces, effective communication serves as the lifeline. Ensuring consistent, clear, and collaborative communication becomes the foundation of successful remote leadership. Virtual becomes real when communication is robust.
- **Prioritizing Technological Integration:** While human touch is irreplaceable, technology is the bridge that facilitates it in a remote environment. A judicious mix of tools can recreate the office experience, fostering seamless collaboration. Technology can bridge the distance.
- **Alignment Through Clarity:** The vastness of the digital realm can sometimes create ambiguity. Leaders must ensure that every team member, irrespective of their location, shares a unified vision and purpose. Distance can blur vision; clarity restores it.

Fostering Connectivity in Virtual Spaces

- **The Power of Active Listening:** In a remote setup, genuine understanding becomes the cornerstone of effective leadership. The nuances of active listening can bridge the emotional and digital gap. Your screen shouldn't mute your empathy.
- **Scheduled Sync-ups:** Regular check-ins foster a sense of unity and belongingness. These sync-ups, while bridging time-zones, also bridge hearts and minds. The periodicity of connection transcends time zones.
- **Collaboration Beyond Boundaries:** The remote envi-

ronment shouldn't limit the collaborative spirit. By fostering a culture of cross-border collaboration, teams can unlock innovations that transcend geographies. Distance is a state of mind.

Crafting a Cohesive Distributed Culture

- **Team Bonding in the Virtual World:** Creating personal connections in a digital realm is an art. Crafting moments that resonate emotionally ensures that team bonds remain unbreakable, irrespective of distance. Digital can also be personal.
- **Promoting Wellness and Balance:** The blurring of work and personal boundaries in remote settings can lead to burnout. Leaders must champion well-being, ensuring that the team remains energized and motivated. A refreshed remote worker is a productive one.
- **Virtual Applause:** In the absence of physical accolades, virtual recognition becomes paramount. Celebrating achievements digitally not only boosts morale but also reinforces the culture of excellence. Celebrating achievements loud and clear.

Quick Thought:
True leadership in a distributed team environment hinges not just on the tools you use, but on how you connect, communicate, and cultivate a shared sense of purpose and community.

Entrepreneurship in Action: Key Ingredients

- **Empathetic Communication:** Understanding and addressing the unique challenges of remote work with empathy and openness.
- **Strategic Technological Adoption:** Leveraging technology not just for operational efficiency but to foster a sense of closeness and community.
- **Culture of Trust and Transparency:** Building a remote work culture where trust is paramount and transparency is a norm, not an exception.

Case Study Highlight: GitLab's All-Remote Culture

Journey of a Bedroom Project: GitLab began its journey as a passion project by its founder, Dmitriy Zaporozhets, who initially developed it as a solution to collaborate on software projects with his team. Little did he know, it would evolve into an industry leader.

No Physical Footprint: GitLab has never had a physical office. This made it a pioneer in showcasing that a company could function, grow, and thrive without centralized brick-and-mortar operations.

Tools and Culture of Trust: It's not just about not having an office; it's about building a culture that thrives remotely. GitLab invested in robust tools for transparency and regular communication, from asynchronous updates to virtual coffee breaks, making remote collaboration as smooth as possible.

Setting the Gold Standard: With detailed documentation on their work processes available publicly, GitLab has set a benchmark on how remote companies should function. They didn't just adapt to remote work; they set the tone for how companies globally could embrace this model.

Remote, Yet Unified: Today, GitLab, with its team spread across multiple countries and time zones, stands as a beacon for organizations aiming to optimize remote work. Their journey underlines the essence of unity without proximity.

```
Pro Tip: In a distributed team, over-communicating
is better than under-communicating. Keep channels
open, conversations frequent, and clarity paramount.
```

Exercise: Distributed Leadership Mastery Workshop

Digital Communication Drill:

- **Tool Evaluation Exercise:** Assess the communication tools currently in use by your team. Gather feedback on their effectiveness and explore new tools that could enhance your team's connectivity. Plan a trial period for one selected new tool.
- **Communication Charter Creation:** Develop a charter that outlines expected communication norms, preferred tools, and response times to ensure clarity and reduce digital miscommunication.

Technology Integration Challenge:

- **Tech-Savvy Team Building:** Identify key areas where

your team's tech skills can be improved. Organize a virtual workshop or a training session with an expert to upskill your team in using collaborative tools effectively.

- **Innovation Hackathon:** Host a virtual hackathon encouraging team members to propose technological solutions or improvements that could streamline remote work processes.

Clarity and Alignment Workshop:

- **Mission and Vision Reiteration Session:** Facilitate a virtual meeting to revisit and reinforce the company's mission and vision, ensuring alignment across all levels of the remote team.
- **Role Clarity Exercise:** Conduct one-on-one sessions with team members to discuss their roles, responsibilities, and expectations, ensuring alignment and addressing any ambiguities.

Remote Culture Building Activities:

- **Virtual Team Bonding Event:** Plan and execute a virtual team-building activity that aligns with your team's interests (e.g., online escape room, virtual talent show). Reflect on its impact on team cohesion and morale.
- **Wellness Initiative Launch:** Start a wellness challenge encouraging team members to share their daily routine of physical or mental health activities, fostering a culture of well-being.

Challenge For You: Over the next month, focus on enhancing one aspect of your remote leadership skills, whether it's improving team communication, fostering a stronger remote culture, or becoming more proficient in the use of a new digital tool. Reflect on the changes and gather feedback from your team on this focused improvement.

Leading Beyond Boundaries: As we navigate the complexities of leading distributed teams, remember that at the core of effective leadership lies the ability to inspire, unite, and lead with conviction, regardless of physical distances. Your leadership can transform remote work challenges into opportunities for growth, innovation, and stronger team cohesion.

Looking Forward: As we delve deeper into the nuances of startup success in the forthcoming chapters, let's embrace the lessons of remote leadership to build teams that are not only productive but deeply connected and engaged, ready to innovate and excel in an ever-changing global landscape.

14

Building a Culture of Innovation

"Innovation is seeing what everybody has seen
and thinking what nobody has thought."
— Dr. Albert Szent-Györgyi

Innovation is the lifeblood of successful startups. To thrive in today's dynamic business landscape, startups must foster a culture of innovation that encourages creativity, empowers employees, and supports the development of groundbreaking solutions. In this chapter, we will delve into the strategies and best practices for building a culture of innovation within your startup. We will explore how to create an environment that nurtures creativity and out-of-the-box thinking, empower employees to contribute their ideas and solutions, and implement structures and processes that support and foster innovation.

In an age where startups spring up daily, innovation is the differentiator that sets the unicorns apart from the crowd. This chapter dives deep into fostering a culture of innovation, ensuring your startup doesn't just adapt, but leads in a dynamic business landscape.

Opening Anecdote: How Adobe Pivoted to Subscription

When software piracy threatened Adobe's revenue, they pivoted. Transitioning from traditional software sales to a subscription-based model, they not only ensured a consistent revenue stream but also provided users with continuous updates and improvements, redefining software delivery.

Creating an Environment that Encourages Creativity and Innovation

- **Mindset Before Skillset:** A foundational understanding of innovation starts with the right mindset. Cultivating a growth perspective allows teams to see beyond challenges, understanding that capabilities can be developed through effort. A company that learns together, innovates together.
- **Fostering Curiosity:** Curiosity is the wellspring of innovation. By encouraging questions and exploration, companies can unearth novel solutions and ideas. Questions today lead to tomorrow's innovations.
- **Collaborative Genius:** Innovation isn't an isolated event; it thrives in collaboration. When diverse minds come together, they can converge their unique insights to birth groundbreaking solutions. Silos are innovation's greatest enemy.

Empowering Employees to Contribute Ideas and Solutions

- **Building Psychological Safety:** Innovation requires vulnerability. When team members feel safe enough to share unpolished ideas without fear of ridicule, the company becomes a breeding ground for innovation. Risk embraced is innovation achieved.
- **Resources for Innovators:** Having an idea is one thing; nurturing it to fruition is another. Providing the necessary resources ensures that creativity isn't stifled but finds a clear path to realization. The best ideas need nurturing.
- **Acknowledging Innovators:** Recognition fuels motivation. Celebrating innovative efforts not only boosts morale but also reinforces a culture where creative thinking is prized. What gets celebrated gets replicated.

Quick Thought:

Innovation thrives not just from individual genius but from a culture that encourages experimentation, embraces failure as a stepping stone, and values diverse perspectives.

Implementing Structures and Processes to Support Innovation

- **Time is of the Essence:** Innovation requires dedicated time. Allocating regular hours for creative endeavors ensures that team members have the space to think beyond the routine. Clock in for innovation.
- **Cross-Functional Think Tanks:** Broadening horizons and perspectives are central to innovation. Cross-

functional teams amalgamate diverse insights, bringing fresh angles to existing challenges. Diversity of thought breeds innovation.

- **Feedback Fuels Refinement:** Innovation is a continuous journey of refining ideas. Embracing feedback at every stage ensures the journey is directed towards viable and impactful solutions. An idea refined is an innovation defined.

Entrepreneurship in Action: Key Ingredients

- **Open Communication:** Ensuring that ideas can flow freely and without barriers across all levels of the organization.
- **Empowered Experimentation:** Giving employees the resources, time, and support to experiment and explore new ideas.
- **Recognition and Reward:** Acknowledging and celebrating innovative contributions, regardless of the outcome, to reinforce the value of creative efforts.

Case Study Highlight: The Continuous Innovation at 3M

Minnesotan Mining Misadventures: 3M, which stands for Minnesota Mining and Manufacturing, began its journey as a mining venture, intending to mine corundum. However, when that venture didn't prove profitable, the founders pivoted to tap into various innovative products. *A*

Culture of Creativity: 3M's success isn't an accident; it's a product of a company culture that allows its employees to spend 15% of their time on projects of their choosing. This "innovation time" led to the invention of some of their most iconic products, such as the Post-it Note.

From Failures to Market-leading Innovations: Not every invention was an immediate hit. The Post-it Note, for instance, didn't find its market until several years after its invention. Yet, 3M's dedication to backing innovative ideas and giving them time to find their audience paid off time and time again.

Driving Innovation: Today, 3M is a multi-industry giant, from healthcare to office supplies. Their journey exemplifies that fostering a culture of creativity and patience can lead to groundbreaking innovations and sustained market leadership.

```
Pro Tip: Innovation isn't just about new products;
it's about improving processes, enhancing
experiences, and challenging norms.
```

Exercise: Innovation Culture Workshop

Innovation Mindset Shift:

- **Growth Mindset Webinar:** Host a session on cultivating a growth mindset, emphasizing resilience and the value of experimentation.
- **Idea Generation Challenge:** Organize a company-wide contest to generate new ideas, providing a safe space for all employees to submit their innovative concepts without fear of judgment.

Curiosity Quest:

- **'Ask Anything' Forums:** Establish monthly forums where employees can ask questions directly to leadership, encouraging curiosity about the company's direction, products, and strategies.
- **Cross-Functional Discovery Days:** Create opportunities for employees to work in different departments for a day, fostering a broader understanding and stimulating innovative thinking.

Collaborative Innovation Labs:

- **Mixed Department Brainstorms:** Facilitate brainstorming sessions that include members from different departments to tackle specific challenges or explore new opportunities.
- **Innovation Project Teams:** Form temporary project teams to explore innovative solutions to internal challenges, encouraging collaboration and a mix of perspectives.

Challenge For You: Over the next month, dedicate time each week to engage in activities outside your normal scope of work to inspire new ideas and perspectives. Share your experiences with your team and encourage them to do the same. Reflect on how these experiences contribute to a broader culture of innovation within your startup.

Cultivating an Innovation Ecosystem: Building a culture

of innovation requires more than just good intentions; it necessitates structured efforts to foster creativity, collaboration, and courage to explore the unknown. By embedding these principles into the DNA of your startup, you pave the way for sustainable growth and continued relevance in an ever-evolving market.

Looking Ahead: As we move forward, our journey will take us deeper into the mechanics of maintaining a thriving startup, focusing on the pillars of operational excellence and legal integrity. Stay tuned for insights on optimizing your operations to support your innovative endeavors and navigating the legal landscape to protect your business and your innovations.

15

Mastering Remote Team Management

"Remote work is not a trend — it's here to stay. Mastering its intricacies will pave the path to global opportunities."
— Luisa Martins

Managing remote teams has become increasingly prevalent in today's business landscape. As companies embrace remote work and distributed teams, leaders must adapt their management strategies to overcome the unique challenges of remote work and foster a productive and cohesive team. In this chapter, we will explore the strategies and best practices for managing remote teams successfully. We will delve into how to overcome challenges such as distance and time zone differences, establish effective communication and collaboration practices, and promote work-life balance and well-being within a distributed workforce.

The digital age has reshaped the realm of teamwork, making managing remote teams a pivotal skill in modern entrepreneurship. In this chapter, we'll dissect the intricacies of remote management, transforming challenges into assets.

Opening Anecdote: The Story Behind Notion's Success

Notion, a collaboration software, grew not only due to its powerful, flexible toolset but also because of its commitment to understanding and facilitating remote work. Their approach to team collaboration and knowledge sharing made them indispensable in a digital age.

Navigating Remote Work Challenges

While remote work offers flexibility and diverse team dynamics, it also brings unique challenges. To effectively navigate this digital terrain, startups need to address the nuances that arise when team members collaborate from different corners of the world.

- **Establishing Clear Guidelines:** Without physical boundaries that an office provides, clear guidelines become the roadmap for efficient remote working. These guidelines remove ambiguity, align efforts, and set the rhythm for virtual collaboration.
- **Bridging Time Zones:** The sun never sets on a distributed team. But this global spread, while offering round-the-clock productivity, also demands strategic planning to ensure smooth collaboration across varied time zones.
- **Fostering Trust & Connection:** Physical distance in remote setups can sometimes translate to emotional distance. It becomes vital to intentionally foster trust and

116

build connections that go beyond work.

> **Quick Thought:**
> *Mastering remote team management is about creating a digital environment where trust, clarity, and empathy flourish, transcending physical barriers to foster a united, productive team.*

Cultivating Communication & Collaboration

In the digital workspace, communication is the glue that holds teams together. Effective collaboration relies on clear, consistent, and open channels of communication.

- **Embracing Digital Communication:** With face-to-face interactions being rare, the nuances of digital communication tools become vital. The right mix can elevate a team's collaboration to new heights.
- **Setting Communication Standards:** While having tools is essential, setting standards for how they're used ensures clarity. A well-defined communication protocol prevents overlaps, misunderstandings, and information silos.
- **Championing Active Listening:** Beyond just communication, truly understanding each other in a remote setting requires active listening. This ensures that despite the digital barrier, team members feel heard and valued.

Championing Work-Life Balance in a Digital Age

In the remote world, the boundary between work and personal life can blur. Championing work-life balance ensures team members remain productive without sacrificing well-being.

- **Empowering Self-Care & Boundaries:** Amid back-to-back virtual meetings and pings, setting boundaries is essential. Encouraging self-care ensures team members feel empowered to recharge.
- **Well-being Resource Provision:** Well-being in a digital age requires different tools. Offering resources that cater to the mental and emotional health of remote workers is imperative.
- **Celebrating Digital Milestones:** Achievements in a remote setting deserve unique celebrations. Recognizing and celebrating these digital milestones can greatly boost team morale and unity.

Entrepreneurship in Action: Key Ingredients

- **Effective Digital Communication:** Choosing the right tools and establishing clear protocols to ensure smooth, clear, and efficient team interactions.
- **Inclusive Scheduling:** Crafting schedules that consider time zones and work preferences to maintain team harmony and productivity.
- **Emphasis on Well-being:** Prioritizing the mental and physical well-being of team members to sustain high levels of engagement and prevent burnout.

Case Study Highlight: The All-Remote Ethos of Buffer

From Bedroom Project to Global Tool: Buffer started as a small project by its founder, Joel Gascoigne, who initially built it to schedule tweets. It quickly morphed into a full-fledged social media management tool as users saw its potential.

Embracing the Remote Model: Buffer, quite early in its journey, decided not to invest in a physical workspace. This decision wasn't just about saving costs but was rooted in a philosophy of work flexibility and global talent acquisition.

Transparent To The Core: Buffer took the idea of transparency to the next level. They publicly shared everything, from their revenue numbers to the salaries of every team member. This cultivated an environment of trust and set them apart in the startup world.

Culture Over Location: With a strong emphasis on team well-being, regular retreats, and allowing members to design their own work routines, Buffer ensured that the absence of an office didn't mean the absence of a strong company culture.

Navigating the Digital Age: Today, as the world moves towards remote work, Buffer's journey offers invaluable insights into building a successful, transparent, and high-trust company without a physical office.

```
Pro Tip: In remote management, presence isn't always
physical. Create an atmosphere where every team
member feels seen, heard, and valued, regardless of
their location.
```

Exercise: Remote Team Mastery Workshop

Digital Workspace Optimization:

- **Tool Evaluation Challenge:** Assess the digital tools currently in use by your team. Gather feedback on their effectiveness and explore new tools that could enhance collaboration and productivity.
- **Virtual Office Setup:** Encourage each team member to share their home office setup in a virtual meeting, discussing tips and best practices for creating an effective work environment.

Time Zone Harmony:

- **Global Clock Project:** Create a shared digital workspace where every team member posts their local time, work hours, and overlaps with others. Use this to plan meetings and collaborative work sessions that respect everyone's time zone.
- **Rotational Meeting Scheduler:** Implement a system where meeting times rotate to share the inconvenience of odd hours equitably, ensuring inclusivity.

Building Virtual Trust:

- **'Meet My World' Sessions:** Host monthly casual sessions where team members share something personal about their culture, hobbies, or local area, fostering personal connections and trust.
- **Feedback Loop:** Initiate a bi-weekly anonymous feed-

back mechanism where team members can share their thoughts on improving remote work practices and team dynamics.

Challenge For You: This month, focus on enhancing one aspect of your remote team management — be it communication, scheduling, or team bonding. Implement targeted improvements, gather feedback, and refine your approach based on the team's input.

Transforming Remote Challenges into Opportunities: Effective remote team management is a blend of technology, empathy, and adaptability. By embracing these principles, leaders can turn the challenge of distance into a testament to their team's resilience and unity.

Looking Ahead: As we continue to explore the multifaceted world of startups, our next chapter will delve into the operational backbone of your venture. Learn how to streamline processes, ensure seamless operations, and maintain a culture of efficiency in a digital-first business environment. Join us as we navigate the operational intricacies that underpin the success of every innovative startup.

16

Performance Management and Feedback

"To manage remotely is to trust deeply; feedback is the compass
that navigates that trust."
— Naomi Shaw

Effective performance management and feedback are crucial for driving the success of remote teams. In this chapter, we will explore strategies and best practices for managing and providing feedback to remote team members. We will discuss setting performance expectations and metrics, providing feedback and coaching in a distributed environment, and recognizing and rewarding the contributions of remote team members.

In the evolving landscape of remote work, performance management and feedback transcend mere metrics. This chapter illuminates the nuances, methodologies, and effective practices for managing and nurturing the growth of remote teams.

Opening Anecdote: Indra Nooyi's Leadership at PepsiCo

Indra Nooyi, former CEO of PepsiCo, stood tall not just as one of the business world's most influential figures but also as a beacon of transformative leadership in a globally dispersed organization. As PepsiCo expanded its footprint across continents, managing diverse and geographically scattered teams became increasingly challenging. Nooyi, however, believed in the pivotal role of feedback in bridging these vast distances. In a move that melded the traditional with the modern, she penned thousands of letters annually to the parents of her employees, expressing gratitude for their invaluable contributions. This gesture, seemingly simple, resonated deeply, underscoring the notion that in the vast expanse of a global enterprise, genuine feedback and recognition can foster unity and cohesion.

Laying the Groundwork: Setting Expectations

A foundation built on clear expectations is vital for remote teams. Without the in-person cues that traditional offices provide, remote workers rely heavily on communicated benchmarks to guide their productivity.

- **Clear Goals are a Remote Worker's North Star:** In the vast sea of remote work, clear goals serve as the North Star, guiding team members and ensuring alignment. Such direction empowers remote workers, ensuring they're contributing effectively and efficiently.
- **Key Performance Indicators - The Pulse of Productivity:** KPIs aren't just numbers; they're the lifeblood of

a business. In remote settings, they serve as a barometer, indicating the health of operations and helping to identify areas of improvement.

Bridging the Distance: Feedback Mechanisms

While technology enables remote work, it's the feedback mechanisms that truly bridge the inherent distance. Effective feedback not only informs improvements but also nurtures relationships in the virtual workspace.

- **Harnessing Technology for Regular Feedback Sessions:** Feedback is the cornerstone of growth, especially in remote environments. Leveraging technology ensures this process is seamless, making the team feel interconnected despite physical distances.
- **Strengths-Based Feedback - A Catalyst for Growth:** In a remote setting, feedback that focuses on strengths acts as a powerful motivator. It not only boosts morale but also encourages team members to further hone their strengths for maximum impact.

> *Quick Thought:*
>
> *Remote performance management transforms feedback from a navigational tool into a bridge that connects and uplifts teams across digital divides, fostering a culture of growth and mutual trust.*

Beyond Metrics: Recognizing and Rewarding Efforts

While metrics provide a quantitative measure, recognizing

and rewarding efforts speaks to the human side of the equation. In a digital age, it's essential to ensure team members feel valued and acknowledged.

- **Digital Acknowledgment Platforms - Celebrating Successes Loud and Clear:** Recognition in the digital realm has its unique flavor. Platforms that celebrate successes ensure that even in remote settings, team members feel the warmth of appreciation and acknowledgment.
- **Tailoring Rewards for the Digital Nomad:** The modern-day digital nomad has distinct preferences and needs. Rewarding them requires a nuanced approach, ensuring what's offered is both relevant and resonates with their unique work lifestyle.

Entrepreneurship in Action: Key Ingredients

- **Clear Communication:** Establishing open lines for honest and constructive feedback, ensuring that expectations are transparent and aligned with company goals.
- **Empathy in Feedback:** Approaching feedback with empathy and understanding, recognizing the challenges of remote work and tailoring feedback to individual circumstances and strengths.
- **Recognition of Effort:** Implementing creative and meaningful ways to recognize and celebrate achievements, reinforcing a positive and motivating work culture.

Case Study Highlight: Intuit's Embrace of Continuous Feedback for Remote Workforce Growth

Initiating a Culture Shift: Intuit, renowned for its financial software solutions like TurboTax and QuickBooks, embarked on a transformative journey to revolutionize its performance management, particularly for its remote workforce. Recognizing the evolving needs of a distributed team, Intuit shifted from traditional annual reviews to a culture of continuous feedback, aiming to foster growth, agility, and responsiveness among its employees.

The Catalyst for Change: The change was sparked by Intuit's realization that annual reviews were too infrequent and retrospective to effectively guide and motivate its diverse and global team. The company sought a more dynamic approach that mirrored its innovative ethos and accommodated the rapid pace of the tech industry.

Implementing Continuous Feedback Loops: Intuit introduced a framework that encouraged regular, real-time feedback among all team members. This approach was designed to not only address challenges promptly but also to celebrate achievements and milestones as they occurred, ensuring that recognition was both timely and relevant.

Tools and Training for Effective Communication: To support this cultural shift, Intuit invested in training its managers and employees in effective communication strategies tailored for remote interactions. This training included mastering digital tools that facilitated seamless feedback and fostering an environment where constructive conversations could thrive, regardless of physical location.

Feedback as a Two-Way Street: A key component of Intuit's strategy was emphasizing that feedback should be a two-way dialogue. Employees were encouraged to seek out feedback proactively and to share their insights and suggestions for improvement with their peers and managers, creating a truly collaborative environment.

The Impact on Team Dynamics: The shift to continuous feedback had a profound impact on Intuit's team dynamics. It led to increased transparency, higher engagement, and a stronger sense of community among remote team members. Employees felt more valued and understood, which in turn, drove higher levels of innovation and productivity.

Recognition and Rewards Evolution: Alongside the feedback overhaul, Intuit reimagined its recognition and rewards system to align with the new focus on continuous improvement. The company introduced more flexible and diverse ways to recognize and reward employees, from peer-to-peer recognition platforms to customized rewards that matched individual preferences and contributions.

Sustaining Growth and Development: Intuit's journey highlights the power of continuous feedback in driving employee growth and development, particularly within remote teams. By embracing this approach, Intuit not only enhanced its operational effectiveness but also reinforced its reputation as a forward-thinking employer that prioritizes the well-being and advancement of its workforce.

Legacy of Innovation in HR Practices: The legacy of Intuit's shift towards continuous feedback and enhanced remote team management extends beyond its immediate benefits. It serves as a blueprint for other companies navigating the complexities of managing distributed teams, illustrating that with the right practices, remote work can be a catalyst for greater employee engagement and organizational success.

This case study exemplifies the profound impact that innovative HR practices can have on a company's culture and performance, particularly in the context of remote work. Intuit's commitment to continuous feedback and employee development sets a benchmark for other startups and established companies alike, showcasing the importance of adapting management practices to meet the evolving needs of the workforce.

Pro Tip: Feedback in remote settings should be timely, specific, and empathetic. Remember, it's not just about managing performance, but fostering growth.

Exercise: Performance Management and Feedback Workshop

Performance Metrics Mapping:

- **Metrics Identification Exercise:** Gather your team to identify critical performance metrics that align with your business goals. Each team member should suggest at least one metric they believe captures their contribution effectively.
- **Alignment and Clarity Workshop:** Host a session to

align these identified metrics with the company's broader objectives, ensuring each team member understands how their work contributes to the overall success.

Feedback Mechanisms for Remote Teams:

- **Feedback Platform Tutorial:** Organize a tutorial on using your chosen feedback platform, highlighting features that facilitate both giving and receiving feedback.
- **Mock Feedback Sessions:** Conduct mock feedback sessions where team members practice giving constructive feedback using the SBI (Situation-Behavior-Impact) model, focusing on clear, actionable insights.

Recognition and Rewards Strategy Design:

- **Recognition Ideas Brainstorm:** Invite team members to brainstorm creative ideas for recognizing and rewarding remote work achievements. Encourage suggestions that go beyond traditional monetary rewards, focusing on personalized and meaningful recognition.
- **Digital Recognition System Setup:** Choose a digital platform for recognition and demonstrate its use to the team, setting up a system for peers to recognize each other's contributions.

Challenge For You: For the next performance review cycle, incorporate a new feedback method focused on strengths and growth. After the cycle, evaluate its impact on team morale and individual performance, adjusting your approach based on feedback from your team.

Navigating Remote Team Dynamics with Feedback: Effective performance management in remote settings isn't just about oversight; it's about fostering a culture where feedback drives development, trust cements collaboration, and recognition fuels motivation.

Looking Ahead: As we delve deeper into the intricacies of remote work, our next chapter focuses on operational excellence in a distributed team setting. Discover strategies to streamline workflows, ensure legal compliance, and maintain a seamless operational flow, setting the stage for sustainable growth and innovation in a digital-first environment. Join us as we explore the foundational elements that ensure your remote team operates like a well-oiled machine, ready to tackle the challenges and opportunities of the digital age.

17

Conflict Resolution and Team Dynamics

"Diversity and open dialogue are the pathways to understanding and growth. In a distributed team, these become even more paramount."
— Dr. Serena Kim

Conflict is an inevitable part of team dynamics, including distributed teams. In this chapter, we will explore strategies and best practices for resolving conflicts in a distributed team, building strong team relationships and trust, and promoting diversity and inclusion in a global workforce. By understanding and effectively managing team dynamics, you can foster a positive and productive work environment for your distributed team.

In a world where digital workplaces reign supreme, conflicts and team dynamics manifest differently. This chapter unravels methods to address disputes, bolster team relationships, and enhance the global inclusivity of distributed teams.

Opening Anecdote: LinkedIn's Evolutionary Growth Story

Reid Hoffman's vision for LinkedIn wasn't just about creating a professional network; it was about understanding the dynamics of professional relationships and growth. Through acquisitions, partnerships, and a deep understanding of its user base, LinkedIn has managed to remain the go-to platform for professionals worldwide.

Navigating Conflicts in Distributed Teams

Remote working, though full of advantages, introduces unique challenges. Just as navigating a ship requires awareness of underwater currents, managing a distributed team requires understanding undercurrents of conflicts that may arise due to distance and cultural differences.

- **The Embrace of Open Communication:** Open communication acts as a safety valve, releasing pent-up issues before they become destructive. It fosters a culture where team members feel valued, understood, and empowered to share without fear of reprisal.
- **Active Listening: More Than Just Hearing:** Listening goes beyond merely hearing words; it's about understanding intent, emotion, and context. In distributed teams, active listening bridges the gap of distance, ensuring everyone feels acknowledged and understood.
- **Mediation: Neutral Ground for Resolution:** Disagreements are natural in any team, but without physical cues, these can escalate quickly in remote settings. Mediation offers a neutral space for resolving conflicts, ensuring that

bridges aren't burned due to misunderstandings.

Cementing Team Trust and Relationships

Trust acts as the glue, holding distributed teams together. Cultivating it requires conscious effort, ensuring team members not only collaborate efficiently but also form bonds that transcend professional boundaries.

- **Crafting Team Norms: The Team's Compass:** Every team has its rhythm and set of unspoken rules. Setting team norms ensures everyone is dancing to the same tune, fostering an environment of mutual respect and shared expectations.
- **Virtual Gatherings: Building Bonds Across Bytes:** Physical distance can lead to emotional distance if not checked. Virtual gatherings act as the campfires of the digital world, where team members gather, share, laugh, and strengthen their bonds.
- **Casual Conversations: The Informal Glue:** While official meetings have their place, it's often the casual conversations that truly bind team members. These informal interactions allow teammates to see beyond the work roles and connect on a human level.

Quick Thought:

Mastering conflict resolution in a distributed team transforms potential discord into harmonious diversity, strengthening the team's collective resilience and creativity.

Championing Global Diversity and Inclusion

Diversity isn't just a buzzword; it's the source of varied perspectives, innovations, and solutions. A team that truly embraces diversity is like a mosaic, where every piece adds its unique color and shine to the bigger picture.

- **Welcoming Varied Perspectives:** Different backgrounds bring unique viewpoints to the table. By welcoming these perspectives, startups not only foster inclusivity but also drive innovation by considering a broader spectrum of ideas.
- **Bias and Stereotypes: Breaking the Shackles:** Every individual has biases, but recognizing and addressing them ensures they don't inhibit collaboration and understanding. Breaking free from these shackles allows a team to truly tap into the power of diversity.
- **Celebrate Diversity Loudly and Proudly:** A team that celebrates diversity doesn't just tolerate differences; it rejoices in them. Recognizing and celebrating these varied backgrounds fosters a culture where every member feels valued and proud.

Entrepreneurship in Action: Key Ingredients

- **Open Communication Channels:** Establishing and maintaining open lines for honest dialogue, ensuring every team member feels comfortable sharing their thoughts and concerns.
- **Active Listening Practices:** Cultivating an environment where active listening is practiced and valued, ensuring team members feel heard and understood.

- **Diversity Celebration:** Actively celebrating cultural diversity and promoting inclusivity, recognizing the unique contributions each team member brings to the table.

Case Study Highlight: Asana's Holistic Approach to Team Harmony

The Genesis of Asana: Asana was born from the challenges Dustin Moskovitz and Justin Rosenstein encountered while managing projects at Facebook. Struggling with the inefficiencies of email for task coordination, they envisioned a platform that could streamline work management and enhance team collaboration. Their mission was clear: to create a tool that enabled teams to work together effortlessly, focusing on the work that truly matters.

Innovating for Team Dynamics: Asana's approach went beyond mere task management; it aimed to transform how teams interact and manage workflows. Recognizing the intricacies of team dynamics, Asana introduced features designed to improve communication, transparency, and accountability. Their platform allowed for seamless integration of various work processes, making it easier for teams to track progress and ensure everyone was aligned with the project's goals.

Holistic Productivity: Asana's platform is a reflection of their deep understanding of not just the tasks but the people performing them. By focusing on clarity and reducing "work about work," Asana helped teams prioritize tasks, manage deadlines, and stay organized without the overload of information that often accompanies project management. This approach to holistic productivity has made Asana a vital tool for companies worldwide, enabling them to achieve more with less stress and confusion.

A Testament to Teamwork: The journey of Asana from a startup to a leading work management platform highlights the power of addressing a common workplace challenge with innovative solutions. Asana's continuous evolution, including the introduction of new features like Timeline and Portfolios, demonstrates its commitment to enhancing team collaboration and productivity. The platform's ability to adapt and grow in response to user feedback and changing work environments has solidified its position as a crucial tool for businesses seeking to navigate the complexities of modern work dynamics.

Cultivating a Culture of Innovation: Asana's success is not just in its technology but also in its culture. The company has fostered an environment where innovation thrives, and every team member feels empowered to contribute ideas. This culture has enabled Asana to stay at the forefront of work management solutions, continually refining and expanding its offerings to meet the evolving needs of its users.

Empowering Teams Globally: Today, Asana is more than just a tool for task management; it's a platform that empowers teams across the globe to work together more effectively. By putting the emphasis on eliminating barriers to teamwork and enhancing communication, Asana has helped countless organizations achieve their objectives more efficiently, proving that thoughtful technology can indeed transform the way work gets done.

Legacy of Leadership: The legacy of Asana is defined by its unwavering focus on improving the way teams work together. As co-founders Moskovitz and Rosenstein continue to guide the company, their leadership exemplifies the importance of vision, adaptability, and a commitment to making work life simpler and more productive. Asana's journey offers invaluable lessons for startups and established companies alike, showcasing that with the right approach, technology can indeed foster harmony, efficiency, and success in any team environment.

> Pro Tip: In distributed teams, the screen can mask emotions. Regularly check in on the well-being of your members, ensuring that they feel seen and heard.

Exercise: Team Dynamics and Conflict Resolution Workshop

Conflict Scenario Role-Play:

- **Scenario Development:** Create realistic conflict scenarios that could occur within remote teams. Include common issues like miscommunication, cultural misunderstandings, or work-style clashes.
- **Role-Playing Sessions:** Organize role-playing activities where team members assume different roles within the conflict scenario. This exercise aims to develop empathy and understanding from multiple perspectives.

Diversity and Inclusion Dialogue Circle:

- **Facilitated Discussion Groups:** Host virtual dialogue

circles focused on sharing cultural backgrounds, personal experiences, and perspectives on diversity and inclusion.

- **Actionable Insights Gathering:** Encourage team members to share actionable insights on how the team can improve its inclusivity practices based on the discussions.

Feedback and Mediation Skill-Building:

- **Feedback Techniques Workshop:** Conduct a workshop on effective feedback techniques tailored for remote environments, emphasizing constructive and strengths-based feedback.
- **Mediation Skills Training:** Offer training sessions on mediation skills to selected team members, empowering them to act as neutral mediators in conflict situations.

Challenge For You: Implement a new initiative aimed at enhancing team dynamics or resolving conflicts within your remote team based on strategies from this chapter. Observe the impact over a month, soliciting feedback from team members to refine your approach further.

Fostering Team Cohesion and Resilience: Effective management of conflicts and nurturing positive team dynamics are critical in a remote setting. By adopting empathetic leadership and inclusive practices, you can build a resilient and cohesive team capable of navigating challenges and leveraging diversity as a strength.

Next Steps: As we progress, the forthcoming chapters will provide deeper insights into achieving operational excellence in a remote setting. Discover strategies for streamlining processes, maintaining quality control, and scaling operations efficiently, ensuring your team operates seamlessly across the digital divide. Join us as we delve into the operational backbone of successful startups, equipping you with the knowledge to optimize your remote team's performance and achieve sustainable growth.

IV

Part Four

Adapting to Change and Building Resilience

18

Taking Calculated Leaps - Risk and Uncertainty

"To succeed in the world of startups, one must dance with
uncertainty and waltz with risk."
— Benjamin T. Wright

Managing risk and uncertainty is a critical skill for entrepreneurs in a global business environment. In this chapter, we will explore strategies and best practices for identifying and mitigating risks, developing contingency plans and risk management strategies, embracing a culture of agility and adaptability, and building resilience to navigate unforeseen challenges.

Navigating the treacherous waters of entrepreneurship requires foresight and agility, especially when managing risks and uncertainties. This chapter arms you with strategies to identify, mitigate, and harness these elements for your venture's growth.

Opening Anecdote: Toyota's Leap into Hybrid Technology

In the wake of 2011, the Fukushima Daiichi nuclear disaster sent shockwaves through many industries. Toyota, a titan of automotive manufacturing, faced significant disruptions in its supply chain due to its lean production system. However, like a phoenix, Toyota rose from this adversity by diversifying its suppliers and fortifying its parts inventory. Their adaptive foresight stands as a beacon for the quintessence of managing risks and uncertainties.

Identifying Threats and Taking Precautions in Global Business Dynamics:

Navigating the unpredictable waters of global business requires a vigilant and proactive stance. Recognizing threats and devising countermeasures help steer the ship safely.

To counteract these challenges, set up workshops emphasizing cybersecurity, ensuring the sanctity of your digital assets. Cultivate relationships with alternative suppliers, ensuring business continuity. Simulate potential threat scenarios to rehearse and refine your response strategies. And as you stride ahead, remember to keep a vigilant eye on the evolving risk landscape. Set up quarterly reviews, stay updated with global business trends, and foster a culture where team members actively share and discuss industry insights.

Strategizing for the "What Ifs":

Uncertainties are a given, but being caught off guard is a choice. The unpredictable nature of business warrants preparedness. Anticipating potential pitfalls helps avoid costly missteps.

Safety nets are paramount. Review your insurance coverage, ensuring every aspect of your venture is protected. Hold workshops delving into risk-transfer mechanisms and consult with industry veterans to glean insights on best insurance practices.

> **Quick Thought:**
> *Embracing risk and uncertainty with a calculated approach transforms potential threats into avenues of growth and innovation.*

Cultivating a Dynamic and Adaptable Culture:

In the world of startups, adaptability is more than a virtue; it's a lifeline. A successful startup thrives on its adaptability. Fostering a culture that welcomes change ensures longevity and growth.

Invest in the team's growth through continuous learning avenues – from industry conferences to online courses, ensuring that the entrepreneurial spirit is always fed with new knowledge and insights.

- **Grit and Recovery – The Resilience Blueprint:** In the sacred halls of entrepreneurship, resilience is often whispered as the unsung hymn. It's not just about navigating rough waters but learning from each wave and dancing in the rain. Endurance and adaptability in the face of challenges define true entrepreneurial spirit. Resilience is about learning, evolving, and persisting.
- **Championing a Growth Attitude:** Every failure is a

foundation stone, a lesson in disguise. Every setback is a potential springboard. A growth attitude ensures that every challenge is seen as an opportunity.

- **Well-being as a Pillar of Strength:** The soul of an enterprise? Its people. The heart of a startup beats through its people. Prioritizing their well-being ensures a harmonious and productive environment.
- **Networking as a Resilience Tool:** Entrepreneurship isn't a solitary journey. The journey of entrepreneurship thrives on connections. Building networks helps share knowledge, gain insights, and create opportunities.

Entrepreneurship in Action: Key Ingredients

- **Proactive Risk Identification:** Regularly scan the horizon for potential risks, using diverse sources and perspectives to catch early warnings.
- **Dynamic Contingency Planning:** Develop flexible contingency plans that can be adapted as situations evolve, ensuring your startup remains agile.
- **Cultural Resilience:** Foster a culture that sees failure as a learning opportunity, encouraging experimentation and innovation.

Case Study Highlight: Dropbox - From Backup Solution to Synchronization Titan

A Eureka Moment in a Bus Station: Drew Houston, the mind behind Dropbox, found himself frequently forgetting his USB flash drive while he was a student at MIT. Frustrated by the inconvenience and the lack of viable solutions, he conceptualized the idea of Dropbox – a tool that could make data universally accessible.

Coding on a Train: With a clear idea in mind, Houston began coding the prototype of Dropbox on a train journey between Boston and New York. He wanted a tool that would seamlessly synchronize data across devices.

Early Skepticism to Viral Launch: While Houston faced skepticism from potential investors and peers initially, a video demo of Dropbox posted on the tech community forum, Hacker News, went viral. This led to thousands of sign-ups overnight and validated Houston's idea.

Not Just Storage, But a Collaborative Tool: Dropbox's success didn't stop at being a backup tool. Recognizing the increasing need for collaborative tools in businesses, Dropbox expanded its services. With features allowing multiple users to work on the same document and share folders, Dropbox transformed into a collaborative workspace.

Facing the Giants: With tech giants like Google and Apple offering their cloud storage solutions, Dropbox faced immense competition. Yet, it was their user-friendly design, seamless integration, and focus on collaboration that helped them carve out a unique niche.

A Symbol of Adaptability and Growth: Today, Dropbox stands as more than just a storage solution. It's a testament to the power of recognizing a personal pain point, innovating a solution, and continuously adapting to meet the ever-evolving needs of the global market. Houston's journey with Dropbox illustrates that with passion, adaptability, and a keen ear to the market's pulse, startups can not only compete with tech giants but also set industry standards.

> Pro Tip: Risk management isn't about avoiding challenges but preparing and leveraging them to your advantage.

Exercise: Risk Management Workshop

Risk Identification Exercise:

- **Scenario Planning:** Break into teams and identify potential risks that could impact your startup in the coming year. Use a broad perspective to consider market changes, operational challenges, and unforeseen global events.
- **Risk Mapping:** Utilize a risk mapping tool to categorize identified risks based on their likelihood and impact. This visual representation helps prioritize risk mitigation efforts.

Contingency Planning Workshop:

- **Strategy Sessions:** For high-impact risks, develop detailed contingency plans. Include clear action steps, responsible team members, and indicators for activating these plans.

- **Simulation Drills:** Simulate a few selected scenarios to test the effectiveness of your contingency plans. Gather feedback from participants to refine and improve.

Adaptability and Resilience Building:

- **Growth Mindset Training:** Conduct a workshop focused on building a growth mindset, emphasizing the importance of adaptability and resilience in the face of challenges.
- **Resilience Circles:** Create small groups to share personal stories of overcoming obstacles, fostering a sense of community and resilience within the team.

Challenge For You: Identify an area within your startup that currently feels vulnerable to unforeseen risks. Implement a risk assessment and develop a tailored contingency plan. After a month, evaluate the plan's effectiveness and adjust based on insights gained.

Navigating Risk with Agility and Insight: Mastering the art of risk management equips you with the tools to steer your startup through the unpredictable tides of the business world. By fostering resilience, encouraging open dialogue about risks, and continuously adapting your strategies, you ensure your venture not only survives but thrives amidst uncertainty.

Next Steps: As we delve deeper into the entrepreneurial

journey, the upcoming chapter on startup marketing will guide you through crafting compelling narratives, leveraging digital marketing tools, and employing strategies that resonate with your target audience in today's fast-paced market. Join us as we explore how to effectively communicate your startup's value proposition, engage with customers, and build a strong, enduring brand.

19

Crisis Management and Business Continuity

"Never let a good crisis go to waste."
— Winston Churchill

In today's dynamic and unpredictable business landscape, entrepreneurs must be prepared to handle unexpected disruptions. Crisis management and business continuity planning are essential components of a resilient and successful startup. This chapter explores strategies and best practices for preparing for and effectively managing crises, developing a crisis response plan and communication strategy, and ensuring business continuity in the face of disruptions.

Emergencies are inevitable, but a startup's survival often hinges on its response. Crisis management and business continuity aren't mere terms but essential lifelines in the entrepreneurial world. Navigate through this chapter to grasp best practices in crisis readiness, robust response planning, and securing your business during tumultuous times.

Opening Anecdote: The Resilience of BlackBerry

Once the go-to for business communications, BlackBerry faced a decline with the rise of smartphones. However, their pivot to cybersecurity and enterprise solutions showcases the resilience of a brand ready to reinvent itself in the face of adversity.

Preparing for and Effectively Managing Crises

When faced with unexpected disruptions, being caught off-guard can be the difference between a temporary setback and an insurmountable challenge. A proactive approach involves mapping out potential threats and formulating actionable responses ahead of time. With the right preparation, your startup can not only weather the storm but emerge stronger and more resilient.

Risk Assessment and Scenario Planning: An entrepreneur's first line of defense is anticipation. By identifying and understanding the potential risks that your startup might face, you're better equipped to develop strategies to manage them. Much like a sailor checking weather patterns before embarking on a journey, these steps ensure you're not blindsided by unforeseen challenges.

Crisis Leadership and Decision-making: Leadership during calm times is different from leadership during crises. In turbulent waters, a team looks up to its captain for direction and assurance. A designated team, trained and equipped to handle emergencies, ensures that panic doesn't set in and that the startup navigates the rough seas with a steady hand and clear vision.

Cross-Functional Crisis Management Team: Crises often stretch across multiple departments. Like a multi-disciplinary medical team treating a patient, each specialist brings a unique perspective and expertise. Combining these ensures a comprehensive, well-rounded response, addressing the crisis from all angles.

> *Quick Thought:*
> *True resilience in business comes from the ability to foresee, adapt, and emerge stronger from crises.*

Crisis Response Plan: The blueprint of any emergency response is the Crisis Response Plan. It's akin to a firefighter's protocol when confronting a blaze - each step clearly outlined, each role defined. Just as architects have blueprints and pilots have flight plans, entrepreneurs need a detailed guide to navigate unexpected challenges, ensuring they act swiftly, decisively, and effectively.

Communication Strategy: In times of crisis, communication isn't just about relaying messages; it's about establishing trust, setting the narrative, and guiding both internal teams and external stakeholders. Much like a ship's captain using both the intercom for the crew and the radio for distress calls, a startup needs an effective strategy to communicate both inwards and outwards during crises.

Media Relations: Media acts as a lens through which the

external world views a crisis unfolding within an organization. Building a healthy relationship with the media is like setting up signal towers - it ensures the messages sent out are clear, accurate, and build trust rather than sow doubt.

Business Impact Analysis: Understanding the domino effect of a disrupted operation or function is crucial. Just as doctors prioritize treating life-threatening injuries first, startups should be equipped to identify and address the most crucial areas of impact during crises.

Remote Work and Technology Infrastructure: The modern digital world allows businesses to operate beyond physical confines. Leveraging this can be a startup's superpower during disruptions. Ensuring that the technological backbone is robust and employees are equipped to work remotely ensures that the business wheel keeps turning, even if the traditional office space is inaccessible.

Supplier and Customer Relationships: Crises can strain the lifelines of a business – its supply chains and its customer relations. Maintaining open channels of communication with suppliers ensures continuity, while transparent dialogue with customers fosters trust. It's akin to keeping both the supply and delivery trucks running smoothly, ensuring the business engine doesn't stall.

Entrepreneurship in Action: Key Ingredients

- **Proactive Crisis Identification:** Stay ahead by regularly assessing potential risks and developing preemptive strategies.

- **Effective Communication:** Establish clear, empathetic, and transparent communication lines for all stakeholders during crises.
- **Adaptive Continuity Planning:** Create flexible business continuity plans that can be rapidly deployed and adapted as situations evolve.

Case Study Highlight: The Transformation of Nokia

Forests, Rubber, and Cables: Nokia's origins trace back to a pulp mill in southwestern Finland. Over the decades, the company ventured into various industries, including rubber, electricity, and cables.

Mobile Revolution: Nokia's foray into telecommunications in the 1960s would set the stage for its meteoric rise as a global leader in mobile phones by the 1990s. The Nokia tune and indestructible phones became cultural icons.

Challenges and Pivots: The arrival of smartphones posed a challenge Nokia couldn't initially overcome. With competitors like Apple and Android taking the lead, Nokia's mobile phone business saw a decline.

Resilience and Renewal: But Nokia wasn't to be counted out. They pivoted, focusing on telecommunications infrastructure through Nokia Networks. Their acquisition of Alcatel-Lucent in 2016 bolstered their position in this sector.

Adapting to Industry Waves: Nokia's storied journey, from its 19th-century beginnings to its modern role in 5G infrastructure, serves as a masterclass in business adaptability, resilience, and the importance of continual evolution in a rapidly changing technological landscape.

> Pro Tip: Crisis communication isn't just about managing external perceptions. Keeping your team informed, reassured, and aligned is equally vital.

Exercise: Crisis Management and Business Continuity Workshop

Crisis Scenario Role-Playing:

- **Scenario Development:** Divide into small groups and develop diverse crisis scenarios that could impact your startup, ranging from natural disasters to cybersecurity breaches.
- **Role-Playing:** Each group presents their scenario to another group, which then role-plays the response using the crisis management strategies discussed in this chapter. Afterward, conduct a debrief to discuss what worked and areas for improvement.

Communication Plan Crafting:

- **Strategy Session:** Work in teams to create a crisis communication plan, identifying key spokespersons, communication channels, and templates for both internal and external messaging.
- **Mock Press Conference:** Simulate a press conference

with a challenging scenario, practicing the delivery of your communication plan and fielding questions from "journalists" played by other team members.

Business Continuity Planning:

- **Business Impact Analysis:** Individually identify critical business functions and conduct a business impact analysis to determine which areas would suffer most in a crisis.
- **Continuity Plan Development:** Use the findings to develop a basic business continuity plan, focusing on maintaining or quickly resuming critical functions.

Challenge For You: Identify a potential crisis that your startup has not yet prepared for. Utilize the insights from this chapter to draft a comprehensive response and business continuity plan. Share this plan with your team for feedback and further refinement.

Navigating Crisis with Strategy and Grace: Effective crisis management and business continuity planning equip your startup to handle unforeseen challenges with confidence. By fostering a culture of preparedness, open communication, and adaptability, you ensure that your venture can withstand, adapt, and grow through any storm.

Next Steps: As you continue to build your startup's resilience, the upcoming chapter on operational excellence will provide you with strategies to optimize your internal processes and systems, ensuring your venture is not only prepared for crises but also operates with efficiency and agility in everyday circumstances. Join us as we explore the foundations of operational excellence and how to apply them to your startup for long-term success.

20

Embracing Innovation and Disruption

"Change before you have to."
- Jack Welch

The winds of innovation and disruption constantly reshape the business horizon. Today's startups not only need to weather these changes but harness them for transformative growth. Dive into this chapter to unearth strategies and real-world examples that underscore the significance of leveraging technological advancements, capturing disruptive trends, and fostering an innovative culture in your startup.

Opening Anecdote: The Rise and Fall of Kodak

Kodak, once synonymous with photography, missed the digital revolution boat, leading to its decline. Their story serves as a stark reminder of the need for businesses to embrace innovation or risk obsolescence.

In the startup ecosystem, the future isn't just a time zone—it's an entity that can be shaped by those who dare to see and leverage upcoming technological trends. It's essential for startups to not just react but proactively anticipate these technological shifts.

Technology Scanning and Trend Analysis: In the ever-evolving landscape of technology, startups must remain vigilant, scanning the horizon for new advancements. This continuous vigilance enables startups to anticipate and adapt to technological changes, ensuring they remain competitive and relevant. By analyzing trends, startups can identify opportunities for innovation, setting the stage for future growth and disruption.

Building Strategic Tech Alliances: Establishing alliances with tech leaders and innovators can provide startups with a competitive edge. These partnerships facilitate access to cutting-edge technology, expertise, and markets, enabling startups to accelerate their growth and enhance their innovative capabilities. Strategic alliances also open doors to collaborative opportunities, driving mutual benefits and fostering a culture of innovation.

Prioritizing Continuous Learning: For startups, the learning curve never flattens. The commitment to continuous education—whether through workshops, courses, or conferences—empowers teams with the knowledge to innovate and adapt. This culture of learning encourages experimentation and risk-taking, essential components of a dynamic and innovative startup environment.

Harnessing Disruptive Technologies and Trends: To truly innovate, startups must not only adapt to current technologies but also seek out and harness disruptive trends. This proactive approach to innovation can redefine industries and create new market opportunities. Startups that successfully leverage disruptive technologies can drive significant change, challenging established norms and setting new standards.

> *Quick Thought:*
> *Embracing innovation is a proactive journey toward future-proofing your startup against inevitable disruptions.*

Market and Consumer Pulse Checks: Understanding the ever-changing needs and behaviors of consumers is crucial for startups aiming to innovate. Regularly engaging with the market and conducting consumer research provides invaluable insights, enabling startups to refine their products and services to meet evolving consumer demands.

The Power of Piloting and Testing: Before committing to a full-scale launch, testing the waters with pilot programs offers startups a low-risk opportunity to validate their innovations. This iterative approach to product development allows for fine-tuning based on real user feedback, increasing the chances of market success.

The Magic of Collaboration: Innovation thrives on diversity of thought and collaboration. By fostering an environment where ideas can freely cross-pollinate, startups can uncover unique solutions to complex problems. Collaboration, both within the team and with external partners, is a key driver of innovation and disruption.

Entrepreneurship in Action: Key Ingredients

- **Continuous Environmental Scanning:** Regularly survey the technological landscape for emerging trends and innovations.
- **Strategic Adaptability:** Develop the agility to pivot strategies based on technological advancements and market needs.
- **Inclusive Innovation Culture:** Foster an environment where every team member is encouraged to contribute ideas and participate in innovation-driven initiatives.

Case Study Highlight: Ayah Bdeir and littleBits - Democratizing Hardware Innovation

Bridging Creativity and Technology: Ayah Bdeir, a Lebanese-Canadian engineer and entrepreneur, embarked on a mission to make electronics accessible and understandable to creators of all ages. Her journey began with littleBits in 2008, a platform of easy-to-use electronic building blocks aimed at democratizing hardware by empowering users to invent anything, from toys to smart home devices, without needing a background in engineering.

The Spark of Innovation: The inception of littleBits was rooted in Ayah's belief in the transformative power of play and experimentation in education. Witnessing a gap between complex engineering concepts and the general public's understanding, she envisioned a system where electronic components could snap together with magnets for prototyping and learning. This led to the creation of littleBits, which quickly became a tool for educators, designers, and hobbyists alike.

Navigating Growth and Challenges: Ayah's journey with littleBits was not without its hurdles. The challenge of balancing educational value with business viability was a constant theme. Moreover, introducing a new category in the toy and education market required not only innovative product development but also strategic partnerships and compelling storytelling to capture the imagination of both children and adults.

Expanding the Horizon: Under Ayah's leadership, littleBits evolved from a novel concept into a community-driven platform, supporting thousands of inventors worldwide. The company fostered an environment of open innovation, encouraging users to share their creations and learn from each other. Ayah's commitment to making technology and engineering accessible to underserved communities, particularly girls and students in STEM, has been a hallmark of littleBits' ethos.

A Legacy of Innovation and Empowerment: Ayah Bdeir's work with littleBits has left an indelible mark on the fields of education technology and hardware innovation. Her focus on intuitive design, community engagement, and inclusive learning has not only propelled littleBits to commercial success but also established Ayah as a pioneer in the maker movement and STEM education. Through her journey, Ayah demonstrates that with vision and perseverance, entrepreneurs can disrupt traditional industries and inspire the next generation of innovators.

Entrepreneurial Insights: Ayah's story is a testament to the power of harnessing technology for social good and the importance of fostering an inclusive culture of innovation. Her approach to problem-solving, prioritizing user experience, and building a community around a product offers valuable lessons for startups aiming to make a lasting impact.

```
Pro Tip: Innovation isn't just about technology;
it's a mindset. Encourage your team to question,
challenge, and think outside the box.
```

Exercise: Innovation and Disruption Workshop

Technological Trend Analysis:

- **Trend Mapping:** Task each team member with researching a specific technological trend that could impact your industry within the next five years. Share findings in a collaborative session.
- **Strategic Application:** Break into groups to brainstorm how these trends could be integrated into your current business model or inspire new product developments.

Disruptive Technology Pilot Program:

- **Pilot Planning:** Select a promising technology identified in your trend analysis. Design a small-scale pilot program to test its applicability and potential impact on your business.

- **Implementation and Review:** Implement the pilot program, closely monitor its progress, and gather data on its effectiveness. Conclude with a review session to evaluate results and decide on future actions.

Cross-Functional Innovation Hackathon:

- **Hackathon Organization:** Host an innovation hackathon inviting all departments to participate. Focus on developing solutions or products that leverage emerging technologies or address upcoming market disruptions.
- **Pitch and Feedback:** Conclude the hackathon with team pitches, followed by feedback from a panel comprising internal leaders and potentially external experts. Reward and plan to further explore winning ideas.

Challenge For You: Identify an area within your startup that could benefit from a disruptive approach or technology. Organize a team brainstorming session to explore innovative solutions, followed by an action plan to test one of these solutions within the next quarter.

Harnessing the Winds of Change: In the fast-paced world of startups, innovation and disruption are not just challenges to overcome but opportunities to be seized. By staying ahead of technological trends, engaging in strategic alliances, and fostering a culture of continuous learning and adaptability, you position your startup at the forefront of industry innovation.

Looking Ahead: As we delve into the entrepreneurial mindset in the next chapter, discover the thought processes, habits, and leadership qualities that empower successful founders to navigate their startups through the complexities of growth and change. Join us in exploring the foundational elements that underpin the resilience and visionary outlook of those who turn challenges into stepping stones for success.

21

Leveraging Data and Analytics for Startups

"Without data, you're just another person with an opinion."
— W. Edwards Deming

In today's data-driven world, startups have a significant advantage if they can effectively leverage data and analytics. This chapter explores strategies and best practices for utilizing data-driven insights in strategic decision-making, implementing data analytics tools and techniques, and leveraging data for process optimization and customer understanding within your startup.

The digital age has conferred startups with a goldmine: Data. However, it's not just about collecting data but extracting actionable insights from it. Dive into this chapter to harness the true potential of data analytics, aiding in strategic decision-making, process optimization, and enhancing customer experiences.

Opening Anecdote: The Analytics Powerhouse: SAS

SAS, a leader in analytics, started at North Carolina State University, aiming to analyze agricultural data. Their deep commitment to analytics has made them an essential tool for businesses aiming to harness data for insights.

In the bustling realm of startups, data acts as the silent whispers guiding the entrepreneur's journey. But to harness its power, one must first lay down clear markers.

Define Key Performance Indicators (KPIs): Establishing KPIs is crucial for measuring success and guiding strategic decisions. These indicators help startups to focus their efforts on what truly matters for growth and sustainability. By setting clear, actionable KPIs, startups can monitor their progress towards achieving their business objectives, allowing for timely adjustments and improvements.

Data Collection and Integration: Effective data collection and integration are foundational to unlocking the power of analytics. By gathering comprehensive data from various sources and integrating this information, startups can gain a holistic view of their operations, customer behavior, and market trends. This integrated data ecosystem is vital for uncovering insights that can drive strategic decisions and foster innovation.

Data Analysis and Visualization: The transformation of raw data into actionable insights is achieved through rigorous analysis and visualization. Tools and techniques for data visualization can illuminate trends, patterns, and anomalies, making it easier for startups to interpret complex datasets. This clarity supports informed decision-making and helps convey findings to stakeholders in an understandable format.

Selecting the Right Analytics Tools: Choosing appropriate analytics tools is essential for extracting valuable insights from data. The right tools can simplify the analysis process, provide real-time insights, and support data-driven strategies. Startups should consider their specific needs, the scalability of tools, and integration capabilities when selecting analytics software.

> *Quick Thought:*
> *In the realm of startups, data isn't just numbers—it's the guiding star illuminating the path to innovation and customer satisfaction.*

Building Analytical Capabilities: Developing in-house analytical capabilities equips startups with the power to harness data effectively. Investing in talent and training for data analysis can elevate a startup's ability to glean insights, predict trends, and make informed strategic decisions.

Embracing Advanced Analytics Techniques: Advanced analytics techniques, such as predictive modeling and machine learning, can offer startups a competitive edge. These techniques enable startups to anticipate customer needs, optimize operations, and identify new opportunities for growth and innovation.

Process Optimization: Leveraging data for process optimization can significantly enhance operational efficiency and customer satisfaction. By identifying bottlenecks and inefficiencies through data analysis, startups can streamline workflows, reduce costs, and improve product or service delivery.

Customer Understanding: A deep understanding of customers, facilitated by data analysis, is crucial for tailoring products, services, and marketing strategies. Insights derived from customer data enable startups to meet and exceed customer expectations, fostering loyalty and driving growth.

Entrepreneurship in Action: Key Ingredients

- **Robust Data Infrastructure:** Establishing a comprehensive data collection and management system that captures all facets of the business operation.
- **Analytical Mindset:** Cultivating a culture where decisions are made based on data-driven insights rather than intuition alone.
- **Continuous Learning and Adaptation:** Staying abreast of the latest in data analytics and technology to continuously refine and adapt strategies based on new insights.

Case Study Highlight: Sheila Lirio Marcelo and Care.com - Harnessing Data to Connect Families and Caregivers

The Inception of Care: Sheila Lirio Marcelo, a Filipino-American entrepreneur, founded Care.com in 2006 out of personal necessity and insight into the broader challenges of finding reliable care solutions. The platform was envisioned as a place where families could meet caregivers not just for children but for elderly relatives and even pets, addressing a universal need across demographics.

Data-Driven Matchmaking: From the outset, Care.com leveraged data and analytics to refine its matching algorithms, understanding that the right caregiver for one family might not be the right fit for another. Through meticulous data collection on both families' needs and caregivers' skills, the platform could offer personalized matches, significantly improving user satisfaction and trust.

Expanding Insights: As Care.com grew, so did its understanding of the care industry's complexities. Marcelo and her team expanded their data analytics capabilities to include insights into care-related trends, regional demand variations, and pricing dynamics. This not only enhanced the platform's utility but also positioned Care.com as a thought leader in the care space.

Challenges and Strategic Pivots: Navigating the intricacies of a marketplace that dealt with something as personal and varied as caregiving services was no small feat. Care.com faced challenges ranging from ensuring safety and trust to managing the logistical aspects of care scheduling and compensation. By continuously refining their data analytics approaches,

Care.com could implement robust vetting processes, introduce safety education resources, and provide transparent pricing information, thereby addressing key user concerns.

Community and Support: Beyond just a platform for finding care, Care.com used data to build a community. They introduced forums and resources guided by user data insights, fostering a supportive network for both families and caregivers. This initiative not only improved user engagement but also reinforced the platform's commitment to addressing the broader aspects of care.

Legacy of Innovation and Social Impact: Today, Sheila Lirio Marcelo is celebrated not only for her entrepreneurial success but for her impact on families worldwide. By prioritizing data-driven decision-making, Care.com transformed how people access care services, making it easier, safer, and more efficient. Marcelo's journey exemplifies how leveraging data and analytics can lead to meaningful innovation that solves real-world problems.

This case study illustrates the power of data in understanding and serving market needs effectively. Marcelo's vision for Care.com, underpinned by strategic use of data analytics, not only created a successful business model but also contributed positively to society by making care more accessible and reliable for millions of users. Her story encourages startup founders to view data as an essential tool for both strategic decision-making and societal contribution.

Pro Tip: Data is potent but remember, always couple data-driven insights with intuitive understanding, especially when it comes to customer experiences.

Exercise: Data Mastery Workshop for Startups

KPI Identification and Dashboard Creation:

- **KPI Workshop:** Gather your team for a workshop aimed at identifying critical Key Performance Indicators (KPIs) that align with your startup's strategic goals. Discuss and finalize a set of KPIs that will guide your decision-making process.
- **Dashboard Design:** Utilize data visualization tools to create dashboards for these KPIs, enabling real-time monitoring. Assign team members to be responsible for updating and analyzing these dashboards regularly.

Data Integration Challenge:

- **Integration Mapping:** Identify various data sources within your startup, from customer feedback to operational metrics. Outline a plan for integrating these disparate data streams into a cohesive analytics platform.
- **Implementation Plan:** Develop a step-by-step action plan to integrate these data sources. Focus on automation where possible to streamline data collection and analysis.

Customer Insights Deep Dive:

- **Segmentation Analysis:** Use your integrated data system to segment your customer base. Identify patterns in customer behavior, preferences, and feedback.
- **Insight Generation:** Based on this segmentation, generate actionable insights that can lead to product improvements, personalized marketing campaigns, or enhanced customer service strategies.

Challenge For You: Identify a recent strategic decision your startup made. Revisit this decision through the lens of the data and analytics tools discussed. Analyze the data relevant to this decision and determine if the insights support the action taken or suggest a different course. Share your findings in a team meeting and discuss the implications for future decisions.

Harnessing Data for Strategic Advantage: By effectively leveraging data and analytics, startups can unlock unprecedented levels of strategic insight, operational efficiency, and customer engagement. Data-driven decision-making becomes the cornerstone of a competitive edge in the fast-paced startup ecosystem.

Looking Ahead: As we explore the operational intricacies of startup success in the next chapter, dive into the strategies that ensure your startup operates like a well-oiled machine. Learn how to streamline processes, implement efficient systems, and maintain agility in operations, ensuring your startup is primed for growth and scalability. Join us as we uncover the operational secrets behind successful startups.

22

Navigating Regulatory and Legal Considerations

"I'm convinced that about half of what separates the successful entrepreneurs from the non-successful ones is pure perseverance"
— Steve Jobs

Understanding regulatory and legal considerations is essential for entrepreneurs to ensure compliance and mitigate legal risks. In this chapter, we will explore strategies and best practices for understanding legal obligations and compliance requirements, protecting intellectual property, and navigating international regulations and cross-border operations within your startup.

Embarking on an entrepreneurial journey comes with its share of regulatory hurdles and legal complexities. Dive deep into this chapter to understand the intricacies of adhering to legal norms, safeguarding intellectual property, and mastering the realm of international regulations.

Opening Anecdote: Sheryl Sandberg, COO of Facebook

Sheryl Sandberg, COO of Facebook, faced a transformative moment during the introduction of the General Data Protection Regulation (GDPR) in Europe. In 2018, while many tech companies scrambled to comprehend and implement the new data protection regulations, Facebook, under Sandberg's guidance, recognized the imperative of GDPR compliance. By initiating transparent dialogues on data privacy, instituting user-friendly data control features, and hosting open sessions on data usage, Facebook aimed to reposition itself as a trusted entity in the data-sensitive European market. Sandberg's foresight not only protected the company from potential regulatory setbacks but also emphasized the significance of proactive legal preparedness in cementing a brand's reputation.

Embarking on the entrepreneurial journey involves more than just innovative ideas and market strategy; it demands a deep understanding of the legal landscape that governs business operations. This chapter, dedicated to navigating regulatory and legal considerations, offers a roadmap for entrepreneurs to ensure compliance, safeguard intellectual property, and successfully manage international regulations and cross-border operations.

Understanding Legal Obligations and Ensuring Compliance (Legal Audits): It's crucial for startups to regularly conduct legal audits to stay ahead of potential regulatory issues. These audits help identify areas of risk and ensure that all aspects of the business are in compliance with current laws, reducing the possibility of costly legal challenges down the line.

Compliance Framework: Establishing a robust compliance framework is essential for startups to manage their regulatory responsibilities effectively. This framework should be designed to adapt to changing laws and regulations, ensuring the startup remains compliant over time.

Education & Training: Educating the team on legal requirements and compliance is not just about risk mitigation; it's an investment in the company's culture of integrity and ethical business practice. Continuous training programs can help keep everyone updated on their legal obligations and the importance of compliance in daily operations.

Intellectual Property Safeguarding: Intellectual property (IP) is often the lifeblood of startups, embodying the unique value they offer. Protecting IP is not merely a legal task but a strategic one that can significantly impact a startup's valuation and competitive edge in the marketplace.

Solidifying Contracts: In the digital age, where partnerships and collaborations span across borders, having solid contracts in place is more important than ever. These agreements protect the startup's interests, outline expectations clearly, and provide a legal framework for resolving disputes.

Risk Mitigation: Effective risk management involves identifying potential legal risks early and developing strategies to mitigate them. This proactive approach can save startups from future legal troubles and financial liabilities.

> **Quick Thought:**
> *In the intricate dance of entrepreneurship, legal and regulatory agility ensures you stay in rhythm, avoiding missteps that could jeopardize your venture's future.*

Abiding by International Laws: For startups looking to expand globally, understanding and complying with international laws is crucial. This includes respecting intellectual property rights across different jurisdictions, adhering to international trade regulations, and understanding the legal requirements for operating in foreign markets.

Protecting IP Internationally: As startups enter global markets, their intellectual property strategy must also scale. This involves securing patents and trademarks in key markets and understanding international IP law nuances to protect against infringement effectively.

Leveraging Local Expertise: Partnering with local legal experts can provide startups with valuable insights into the regulatory environment of new markets. These partnerships can help navigate local laws more effectively, ensuring compliance and minimizing legal risks during international expansion.

Entrepreneurship in Action: Key Ingredients

- **Proactive Legal Planning:** Establishing ongoing legal

audits and compliance checks to pre-emptively address potential legal issues.

- **Intellectual Property Vigilance:** Actively protecting and managing intellectual property to safeguard and capitalize on your startup's innovations.
- **Global Compliance Mindset:** Understanding and navigating the complexities of international laws and regulations to ensure seamless global operations.

Case Study Highlight: Jessica O. Matthews and Uncharted Power - Revolutionizing Energy through Innovation

The Spark of Innovation: Jessica O. Matthews, a Nigerian-American inventor, and entrepreneur, founded Uncharted Power as a sustainable energy company with a mission to democratize energy access worldwide. Her journey began with an insight during her aunt's wedding in Nigeria, where she experienced firsthand the disruptive impact of unreliable power supply. This experience ignited a passion to create solutions that harness kinetic energy for electricity generation.

The Ethical Commitment: Matthews' commitment to sustainability and innovation was evident from her first invention, the SOCCKET ball - a soccer ball that generates electricity when kicked around. This invention wasn't just a product; it was a testament to Matthews' dedication to blending technology, social good, and environmental sustainability. Uncharted Power's ethos centered around creating scalable, sustainable energy solutions that empower communities without harming the planet.

Challenges and Adaptation: As Uncharted Power evolved,

it faced the challenges inherent in pioneering new technology and disrupting established energy markets. Matthews navigated these challenges by focusing on research and development, securing patents for her company's unique technology, and forming strategic partnerships with municipalities and utility companies. Her ability to pivot and adapt was crucial as she worked to bring her vision of sustainable, accessible energy to life on a global scale.

Beyond Energy - Building Smart, Sustainable Infrastructure: Recognizing the broader implications of energy access, Uncharted Power expanded its focus to include the development of smart infrastructure solutions. The company's platform uses advanced data analytics to improve efficiency in energy distribution and consumption, aiming to build smarter, more resilient communities. This holistic approach underscores Matthews' vision of technology as a tool for systemic change.

Legacy of Innovation and Responsibility: Today, Jessica O. Matthews stands as a beacon of innovative and ethical entrepreneurship. Uncharted Power's success story is not just about technological breakthroughs; it's about envisioning a future where business success and social impact go hand in hand. Matthews' journey from an inspired inventor to the leader of a groundbreaking energy company exemplifies how commitment to ethics and social responsibility can drive transformative change.

Through her pioneering work, Matthews has not only contributed to the field of renewable energy but has also inspired a new generation of entrepreneurs to pursue ventures that are profitable, innovative, and aligned with the greater good.

Her legacy is a powerful reminder of the impact that visionary leadership, combined with ethical business practices, can have on the world.

In reflecting on Uncharted Power's journey, startup founders can glean valuable insights into the importance of aligning business objectives with ethical considerations and the potential for innovation to address global challenges. Jessica O. Matthews' story exemplifies how navigating regulatory and legal considerations with a commitment to social responsibility and environmental sustainability can propel a startup to global success while making a lasting positive impact.

Pro Tip: Engaging in legal compliances isn't just about avoiding fines; it's about building trust and a positive brand reputation in the market.

Exercise: Legal and Regulatory Readiness Workshop

Legal Audit Simulation:

- **Mock Audit:** Conduct a simulated legal audit of your startup. This exercise involves reviewing current compliance with industry regulations, privacy policies, employment laws, and intellectual property rights.
- **Action Plan:** Based on the findings, develop an action plan to address any gaps in compliance. Assign responsibilities to team members for implementing necessary

changes.

International Expansion Scenario Planning:

- **Market Entry Strategy:** Choose a new market your startup is considering entering. Research and discuss the regulatory environment of this market, focusing on specific challenges and opportunities.
- **Compliance Roadmap:** Craft a detailed plan for achieving compliance in this new market, including steps for intellectual property protection, data privacy adherence, and local legal requirements.

IP Protection Workshop:

- **IP Inventory:** Create an inventory of all current and potential intellectual property assets within your startup. This includes patents, trademarks, copyrights, and trade secrets.
- **Protection Strategies:** For each identified IP asset, discuss and outline the best strategies for protection, both domestically and internationally. Consider engaging with IP legal professionals for deeper insights.

Challenge For You: Reflect on a recent strategic move or product launch within your startup. Evaluate this decision from a legal and regulatory perspective. Identify any potential risks you may have overlooked and propose a plan to mitigate these risks in the future.

Navigating Regulatory and Legal Considerations: Mastery

of legal obligations and compliance requirements is not just a defensive strategy—it's a competitive advantage that protects and propels your startup forward.

Looking Ahead: As we transition into the operational core of startup success, prepare to delve into the essentials of efficient operations management. Discover strategies for resource allocation, process optimization, and maintaining agility in your startup's operations. Join us in the next chapter to solidify the foundation upon which your startup's success is built.

V

Part Five

Building Sustainable Success and Impact

23

Sustainable Business Practices

"What we do today echoes in eternity."
— Marcus Aurelius

In today's fast-paced entrepreneurial world, sustainability emerges not just as a noble endeavor but as a cornerstone of smart business. When startups choose to thread sustainable practices into their business tapestry, they don't just champion global causes; they build resilient, future-proof enterprises. This chapter dives deep into integrating sustainability seamlessly into startup strategy, practices, and ethos.

Opening Anecdote: The Ethical Coffee Supply Chain of Starbucks

Starbucks, beyond its global coffeehouse chain status, has been a leader in promoting ethically sourced coffee. Their commitment to farmers and sustainable practices showcases how businesses can be profitable while also being socially responsible.

Crafting a Sustainable Business Strategy:

Environmental Impact Assessment: Understanding the environmental footprint of your startup is the first step to making informed decisions. It's about acknowledging how your operations affect the planet.

Social Impact Considerations: A startup's reach extends beyond profit margins. It influences communities, economies, and societies at large. Assessing social impact ensures that your startup contributes positively to societal frameworks.

Sustainable Supply Chain Management: Your supply chain—the network of suppliers, manufacturers, and distributors—is a pivotal aspect of your startup's ecological and social imprint. Ensuring it aligns with sustainable goals reinforces your brand's ethical stance.

> **Quick Thought:**
> Sustainability isn't just an ethical choice; it's a strategic advantage that can distinguish your startup in a crowded

marketplace.

Implementing Environmentally and Socially Responsible Practices: Beyond mere compliance, championing responsible practices boosts brand image, cultivates trust, and can even enhance operational efficiency.

Engaging Stakeholders in Your Sustainable Vision: Stakeholders, from investors to customers, increasingly prioritize sustainability. Involving them not only secures buy-in but fosters collaborative progress.

Building a Business with Impact at its Core: A mission transcending profit can serve as a magnetic north, guiding and grounding your startup's endeavors. This core purpose can be the driving force behind every decision.

Entrepreneurship in Action: Key Ingredients

- **Proactive Environmental Stewardship:** Emphasizing renewable energy, waste reduction, and sustainable sourcing to minimize environmental impact.
- **Social Responsibility:** Actively contributing to societal well-being through community engagement, ethical labor practices, and inclusive policies.
- **Sustainable Innovation:** Continually seeking innovative solutions that reduce ecological footprints while addressing market needs.

Case Study Highlight: Ecosia - The Search Engine Planting Trees

In a world dominated by tech giants, the Germany-based Ecosia emerged as a unique and eco-friendly alternative. On the surface, Ecosia might look like any other search engine, but what sets it apart is its commitment to sustainability and its promise to use the profits from search ads to plant trees.

From Concept to Green Impact: Founded by Christian Kroll in 2009, the idea was ignited by a trip around the world. Witnessing deforestation and understanding the vital role of trees in our ecosystem led to the birth of Ecosia. The vision was clear - to tackle both information access and environmental degradation.

Transparent Operations: Ecosia's commitment to transparency is exemplary. They release monthly financial reports, ensuring users know exactly where their money goes. Almost 80% of their surplus income goes directly into tree-planting projects, amounting to millions of trees every month.

Beyond Just Trees: While tree planting remains their core focus, Ecosia's reach has expanded. Their profits also support various global projects, from reforestation in Brazil to providing clean drinking water in Uganda. Moreover, their server infrastructure runs on 100% renewable energy, marking a holistic approach to environmental responsibility.

A Model of Sustainable Tech: Despite facing stiff competition from leading search engines, Ecosia has carved a niche, boasting millions of active users. It's a testament that technology and sustainability can blend seamlessly, offering users a chance to make a difference with their everyday actions.

The Takeaway: Ecosia stands as a beacon, proving that

businesses can embed sustainability at their core, and in doing so, create a ripple effect of positive change across the globe.

Pro Tip: Make sustainability the lifeblood of your
business, allowing it to guide decisions,
operations, and long-term visions.

Exercise: Sustainability Integration Workshop

Environmental Footprint Analysis:

- **Activity:** Conduct a comprehensive analysis of your startup's environmental footprint, focusing on areas such as energy consumption, waste generation, and resource utilization.
- **Outcome:** Develop a plan to reduce the environmental impact, including setting tangible, achievable goals for energy efficiency, waste reduction, and sustainable resource use.

Social Impact Assessment:

- **Activity:** Evaluate the social impact of your startup on the community, employees, and other stakeholders. Identify areas where your business operations can contribute positively to societal issues.
- **Outcome:** Create initiatives or partnerships that enhance your startup's contribution to social welfare, such as

community development programs or fair labor practices.

Sustainable Supply Chain Development:

- **Activity:** Assess the sustainability of your current supply chain. Identify areas for improvement, such as sourcing from ethical suppliers or reducing the carbon footprint of logistics.
- **Outcome:** Implement a sustainable supply chain strategy that includes criteria for selecting eco-friendly suppliers and methods for minimizing logistics-related emissions.

Challenge For You: Reflect on a product, service, or operation within your startup. Identify how it could be redesigned or reimagined to enhance sustainability. Share your ideas with your team and explore their feasibility and potential impact.

Sustainable Business Practices: Embracing sustainable practices is not just about future-proofing your business against environmental and social challenges; it's about leading by example and inspiring change in your industry and community.

Looking Ahead: As we transition into the operational essentials for startup success, prepare to explore strategies for streamlining processes, maintaining compliance, and optimizing resource allocation. Join us in the next chapter to fortify your startup's operational framework, ensuring efficiency, agility, and sustainability in every endeavor.

24

Entrepreneurial Ethics and Corporate Social Responsibility

"I can accept failure, everyone fails at something. But I can't accept not trying."
— Michael Jordan

The fabric of successful startups is woven with ethical considerations and a sense of responsibility. As you delve into this chapter, you'll uncover the importance of fostering an ethical business environment, engaging in impactful corporate social responsibility (CSR) initiatives, and striking a balance between profitability and conscientious considerations.

In today's competitive startup environment, maintaining ethical integrity and embracing social responsibility are more than just virtuous pursuits; they're essential for long-term survival and success. As budding entrepreneurs, understanding how these principles align with profitability can shape your startup's legacy.

Opening Anecdote: The Green Energy Pursuits of IKEA

IKEA's vision isn't limited to affordable furniture; it's about a sustainable future. Their investment in renewable energy and commitment to a circular economy showcases how businesses can pave the way for a greener tomorrow.

Promoting Ethical Business Practices and Responsible Leadership

- **Ethical Decision-Making:** Ethics is the compass guiding every business decision. It entails making choices that reflect the core values and principles of your startup, even when they're tough.
- **Stakeholder Engagement and Accountability:** Stakeholders, including employees, investors, and customers, rely on your startup's ethical stand. Keeping them in the loop solidifies trust and paves the way for mutual growth.
- **Responsible Leadership:** Leadership sets the tone for an organization's ethical climate. Leading with integrity ensures a ripple effect, with employees emulating these standards.

> *Quick Thought:*
> *Ethical practices and CSR initiatives are not just moral choices; they are strategic business decisions that can drive long-term success and differentiation in the market.*

Engaging in Corporate Social Responsibility Initiatives

- **Identifying CSR Priorities:** CSR initiatives should resonate with your startup's mission, vision, and stakeholder
expectations. A well-defined focus ensures meaningful
impact.
- **Partnerships and Collaboration:** Collaborating with
external entities can amplify the impact of CSR initiatives.
Partnerships bring expertise, resources, and fresh perspectives.
- **Measurement and Reporting:** Measuring the outcomes
of CSR efforts ensures transparency and highlights areas
of improvement.

Balancing Profit with Social and Environmental Consid-
erations

- **Triple Bottom Line Approach:** Modern startups don't
just focus on financial profits. They also account for
their social and environmental impacts, ensuring holistic
growth.
- **Sustainable Supply Chain:** Your supply chain, from raw
materials to end product, should mirror your ethical and
sustainable principles.
- **Product and Service Innovation:** Innovative products
and services that prioritize sustainability cater to an ever-
growing conscious consumer base.

Entrepreneurship in Action: In 2009, Brian Chesky, one
of the co-founders of Airbnb, found himself amidst a PR
disaster. Some hosts had their homes vandalized, which

raised questions about Airbnb's safety measures. Instead of deflecting blame or minimizing the situation, Chesky openly admitted the company's shortcomings and introduced a comprehensive $1 million host guarantee. By addressing the issue ethically and transparently, Airbnb illustrated that startups can effectively navigate crises by upholding their core values.

Entrepreneurship in Action: Key Ingredients

- **Integrity in Leadership:** Leading by example, where leaders demonstrate commitment to ethical practices and social responsibility.
- **Engagement and Transparency:** Actively involving employees, customers, and stakeholders in ethical decision-making and CSR initiatives.
- **Innovation for Good:** Leveraging innovation not only for business growth but also to address social and environmental challenges.

Case Study Highlight: Blake Mycoskie and TOMS Shoes - Buy One, Give One

The Genesis of an Idea: During a trip to Argentina, Blake Mycoskie saw children without shoes and was deeply moved. This experience gave birth to TOMS Shoes, which operated on a unique model: for every pair sold, another pair would be given to a child in need.

The Ethical Commitment: Instead of merely capitalizing on the buy-one-give-one model as a marketing strategy, TOMS genuinely committed to it. They worked with local

NGOs to distribute shoes and later expanded their offerings to eyewear, coffee, and bags, addressing additional needs like sight and clean water.

Challenges and Adaptation: As TOMS grew, so did criticism. Some argued that free shoes could hurt local businesses. In response, TOMS adapted by starting to produce a portion of their giveaway shoes in the countries where they were donated, thus creating jobs and supporting local economies.

Beyond Shoes - A Holistic Approach: Recognizing the broader challenges faced by communities, TOMS diversified their giving approach, addressing issues like eyesight, clean water, and safe births. They incorporated feedback, showcasing the adaptability of startups to evolve ethically.

Legacy of Ethical Entrepreneurship: Today, TOMS stands as an exemplar of how businesses can meld profit with purpose. Mycoskie's journey underscores that with a strong ethical foundation, startups can make lasting societal impacts while thriving in the marketplace.

```
Pro Tip: Ethics and CSR aren't about gaining
short-term publicity. They represent a startup's
genuine commitment to the larger good.
```

Exercise: Ethical and CSR Strategy Workshop

Ethical Framework Establishment:

- **Activity:** Develop an ethical code of conduct tailored to your startup's unique culture and values. Involve your team in the drafting process to ensure buy-in and understanding.
- **Outcome:** A comprehensive ethical guideline that informs decision-making processes, shapes company culture, and sets clear expectations for ethical behavior.

CSR Initiative Planning:

- **Activity:** Identify a social or environmental issue closely aligned with your startup's mission. Brainstorm and plan a CSR initiative that addresses this issue while engaging your team and stakeholders.
- **Outcome:** A detailed plan for a CSR project, including objectives, expected impact, involved parties, and metrics for success. This initiative should also include methods for stakeholder engagement and transparency.

Sustainability Audit:

- **Activity:** Conduct an audit of your startup's operations to identify areas where you can implement more sustainable practices. Focus on supply chain, energy use, waste management, and social impact.
- **Outcome:** An actionable sustainability improvement plan with specific goals, timelines, and responsible parties. This plan should aim to reduce your environmental footprint and enhance your social contributions.

Challenge For You: Conduct an "Ethics Day" at your startup, where you and your team explore ethical dilemmas related to your industry. Discuss potential scenarios, decisions, and their implications to foster a deeper understanding and commitment to ethical practices.

Entrepreneurial Ethics and CSR: Embedding ethical considerations and social responsibility into your startup's DNA ensures that your business contributes positively to society while building a solid foundation for long-term success.

Looking Ahead: As we move forward, delve into the operational essence of startups. Explore how strategic planning, efficient resource allocation, and effective process management can propel your startup towards operational excellence and sustainable growth. Join us in the next chapter to unlock the operational strategies that underpin successful startups.

25

Crafting the Grand Finale - Exit Strategies and Leaving a Legacy

"In the end, it's not the years in your life that count. It's the life in your years."
— Abraham Lincoln

Planning for a successful exit is a crucial consideration for startup founders. In this chapter, we will explore various exit options and strategies for startup founders, discuss the importance of planning for a successful exit or succession plan, and explore ways to build a lasting legacy and give back to the entrepreneurial community.

Even as a startup founder revels in the journey, considering a graceful exit and leaving a lasting impact is paramount. Dive into this chapter to discover the world of strategic exits and the art of building an enduring legacy.

Opening Anecdote: The Visionary Legacy of Steve Jobs at Apple

Steve Jobs wasn't just a tech visionary; he was a storyteller. His return to Apple and the subsequent launch of products like the iPod, iPhone, and iPad transformed industries. However, his most significant legacy was the culture of innovation he instilled, ensuring Apple's continued success even post his era.

Mastering The Exit - Options and Pathways

Every business, no matter how personal, may eventually face the prospect of an exit. And in these crucial junctures, informed choices make all the difference.

- **Initial Public Offering (IPO):** Basking in the limelight of the stock market can elevate a startup to unprecedented heights. The allure of the stock market can elevate a startup's stature and potential. Navigating its intricacies ensures the spotlight shines favorably.
- **Merger or Acquisition (M&A):** M&As can be game-changers, ushering startups into larger playing fields. The dance is delicate, but the rewards vast.
- **Management Buyout:** Sometimes, leadership from within promises a startup's brightest future. Trusting the known can be a visionary move.
- **Strategic Alliances:** Collaborations might just be the ticket to new opportunities without a complete exit. Partnerships can unlock doors without ceding control. Collaborate to co-create and scale.

Seamless Transition – Planning for Exit & Succession

The baton change in a startup's relay race is crucial. Make it smooth and intentional. Every leader steps down, but the legacy remains. Make the transition graceful and impactful.

- **Exit Blueprinting:** A premeditated exit is a graceful one. Plan for it.
- **Passing the Torch - Succession Planning:** A founder's legacy is often seen in the successors they groom. Legacy is not just what you leave, but whom you prepare.
- **Navigating the Legal Labyrinth:** Legal missteps during exits can be costly. Tread with caution. Exits bring legal intricacies. A misstep can be pricey.

Quick Thought:

A well-planned exit and a thoughtful succession strategy are the keystones of a lasting legacy. They reflect the foresight, responsibility, and ethical stewardship of a leader.

Beyond Business - Crafting a Legacy & Giving Back:

The journey doesn't end with an exit; sometimes, it's just the beginning. The entrepreneur's journey often transcends business. Leave a mark, inspire and uplift.

- **Mentorship - Guiding the Next Wave:** Your experiences are tomorrow's lessons. Share and shape futures.
- **Philanthropy - The Heart of Entrepreneurship:** Business is just one way to touch lives; explore the power of giving. Beyond profit lies purpose and you can make a

difference.

- **Advocacy & Thought Leadership:** Be the lighthouse in the entrepreneurial storm. Guide, inspire, and set standards.

Entrepreneurship in Action: Key Ingredients

- **Strategic Vision:** Understanding the end game and planning your exit or succession with the same zeal as the startup phase.
- **Ethical Leadership:** Making decisions that not only benefit the startup but also consider the impact on employees, stakeholders, and the community.
- **Community Contribution:** Building a legacy that transcends business success to include contributions to societal and environmental well-being.

Case Study Highlight: Janice Bryant Howroyd and ACT-1 Group - Pioneering Workforce Solutions with Integrity

The Genesis of Empowerment: In 1978, Janice Bryant Howroyd, armed with $1,500, a passion for people, and an unwavering belief in the power of talent, founded the ACT-1 Group in a small office in Beverly Hills, California. Her vision was clear: to revolutionize the staffing industry by prioritizing the human element in every professional engagement.

The Ethical Commitment: From the onset, Howroyd was determined to build her company on a foundation of integrity and respect. The ACT-1 Group, under her leadership, not only focused on connecting individuals with meaningful work but also on ensuring fair labor practices and championing diversity and inclusion. This commitment extended beyond her company, influencing the staffing industry as a whole to consider more equitable and humane practices.

Challenges and Adaptation: As the ACT-1 Group expanded, it faced the growing pains typical of any burgeoning enterprise. However, Howroyd's challenges were compounded by the barriers she faced as a woman of color in a predominantly male-dominated industry. Despite these obstacles, her resolve only strengthened. Howroyd adapted by leveraging her unique perspective to innovate within her field, ultimately distinguishing the ACT-1 Group as a leader in workforce solutions.

Beyond Staffing - A Holistic Vision: Recognizing the evolving needs of the global workforce, Howroyd expanded her company's services to include broader HR solutions, vendor management, and business consulting, thus addressing the comprehensive needs of both workers and corporations. Her approach was not just about filling positions but empowering individuals and organizations to achieve their full potential.

Legacy of Inclusive Entrepreneurship: Today, Janice Bryant Howroyd stands as the first African American woman to build and own a billion-dollar company. Her journey from a small-town girl to a global business titan is a testament to the power of ethical entrepreneurship. The ACT-1 Group's continued success is a beacon for how businesses can flourish by prioritizing integrity, respect, and the well-being of the community.

Through her pioneering spirit and ethical business practices, Howroyd has not only built a lasting legacy for herself but also set a benchmark for future entrepreneurs to aspire toward.

Her life's work underscores the belief that business success and social responsibility can go hand in hand, inspiring a new generation of entrepreneurs to build their enterprises on a foundation of integrity and community impact.

```
Golden Nugget: Exiting is not about ending; it's
about evolving. Ensure this evolution resonates with
the ethos of your venture.
```

Exercise: Legacy Planning Workshop

Exit Strategy Simulation:

- **Activity:** Map out various exit scenarios for your startup, including an IPO, acquisition, or strategic partnership. For each scenario, outline the steps, potential challenges, and how you would navigate these challenges.
- **Outcome:** A comprehensive understanding of possible exit strategies, preparedness for different scenarios, and a strategic plan that aligns with your long-term goals and values.

Succession Planning Exercise:

- **Activity:** Identify potential successors within your organization or outline the qualities and skills you would seek in an external successor. Develop a mentorship and transition plan to prepare for a seamless leadership handover.

- **Outcome:** A clear succession plan that ensures the continuity and stability of your startup, with a timeline and process for mentoring and empowering your successor.

Philanthropy and Giving Back Strategy:

- **Activity:** Choose a cause or community initiative relevant to your startup's mission. Design a philanthropy strategy that integrates this initiative into your business model, including partnerships, funding, and employee engagement.
- **Outcome:** A detailed philanthropy strategy that not only contributes to a cause but also enhances your startup's brand and legacy, fostering a culture of giving and community involvement.

Challenge For You: Reflect on your startup's impact beyond the balance sheet. Initiate a legacy project that aligns with your values and mission, whether it's a mentorship program, a sustainability initiative, or community service. Document the planning process, the implementation challenges, and the outcomes.

Entrepreneurial Ethics and Corporate Social Responsibility: Fostering an environment of ethical business practices and social responsibility not only shapes your startup's culture but also sets a foundation for lasting impact and a meaningful legacy.

Looking Ahead: As you continue on your entrepreneurial

journey, remember that the operations, strategies, and decisions of today shape the legacy of tomorrow. Let this guide be a compass as you navigate the complexities of building a successful, ethical, and impactful startup.

Epilogue: Unleashing the Extraordinary

As we embark upon the culmination of this extraordinary odyssey, a tapestry of awe-inspiring insights unfolds before us. With each turn of the page, we have delved into the depths of entrepreneurial wisdom, harnessing its transformative power. Now, as we conclude this remarkable chapter, let us reflect on the journey that has brought us here and discover the resounding echoes of greatness that reverberate within.

Recap of Key Takeaways and Insights from the Book: Behold the kaleidoscope of wisdom that has graced our voyage, illuminating the path to entrepreneurial excellence. From the lofty peaks of startup strategy to the vast horizons of leadership and management, we have traversed a landscape teeming with invaluable lessons. We have witnessed the alchemy of innovation, the artistry of marketing, and the symphony of personal growth. In the tapestry of finance, investment, and risk, we have discovered the delicate dance that fuels entrepreneurial dreams. And as we gaze upon the mosaic of success stories, we find inspiration and courage to forge our own destinies.

Encouraging Ongoing Learning and Adaptation in En-

trepreneurship: Yet, let us not rest upon the laurels of knowledge acquired. The entrepreneurial spirit thrives on an insatiable thirst for wisdom. In a world that spins with perpetual motion, adaptation is the currency of progress. It is in the relentless pursuit of learning that we unlock the door to boundless opportunity.

Embrace the fervor of curiosity, where the boundaries of the known yield to the allure of the unexplored. Seek enlightenment in the company of visionaries, draw inspiration from diverse perspectives, and dare to challenge convention. Let the symphony of innovation be your guiding melody as you conduct the ever-evolving symphony of your entrepreneurial journey.

Empowering Entrepreneurs to Navigate the Global Workforce and Achieve Long-Term Success: In the realm of the global workforce, the tapestry of entrepreneurship spans continents, connecting hearts and minds in a tapestry of boundless possibilities. Armed with the brush of leadership, paint upon the canvas of remote teams a masterpiece of collaboration and synergy.

Unleash the power of effective communication, transcending borders and cultures with the eloquence of understanding. In the crucible of cross-cultural encounters, embrace the richness of diversity and weave it into the fabric of your leadership. Adorn yourself with adaptability and cross the thresholds of the global marketplace with confidence. For it is through the harmonious orchestration of the global workforce that you shall manifest enduring success.

Embracing Resilience and Building a Supportive Com-

munity: As twilight descends upon the entrepreneurial path, challenges emerge as the crucibles of resilience. With every setback, a wellspring of strength awaits, beckoning you to rise above the tempest and forge ahead with unwavering determination.

Yet, in the labyrinth of entrepreneurship, you need not traverse the maze alone. Surround yourself with kindred souls, mentors, and guides who illuminate the darkest of hours with their wisdom and support. Forge bonds of camaraderie, where collaboration gives birth to miracles. For it is in the embrace of a supportive community that triumphs are magnified, and the echoes of your achievements resonate through the ages.

Conclusion: In the tapestry of this awe-inspiring journey, the chapters have unfolded, unveiling the secrets of entrepreneurial mastery. The threads of knowledge, insights, and best practices have woven together a fabric that envelops you, empowering you to seize the reins of destiny.

After chronicling this odyssey, I reflect upon my journey in crafting this guide. Every word, every insight, was derived from a tapestry of personal experiences, learnings from mentors, and a desire to see each one of you succeed. As you progress in your entrepreneurial journey, remember that while the tools and landscapes might evolve, the principles of entrepreneurship stand eternal and true.

Now, as we conclude this symphony of wisdom, let the crescendo of action reverberate within your soul. Apply the tapestry of lessons to your entrepreneurial endeavors with boldness and tenacity. Embrace the unknown, for it is there that the extraordinary awaits. And as you venture forth, remember that the world is your canvas, awaiting the strokes of your brilliance.

Unleash the extraordinary within you, for the entrepreneurial spirit knows no bounds. Let the symphony of your achievements resound across the ages, inspiring generations yet to come. As we bid farewell, may your path be illuminated by the radiance of your dreams, and may your entrepreneurial journey be an awe-inspiring testament to the limitless power of the human spirit.

Lastly, from the depth of my heart, thank you for embarking on this journey with me. It is my sincere hope that this book serves as a trusted companion on your path to extraordinary success.

The Ask

Dear Global Trailblazer,

Did your journey through the pages of this guide spark a newfound ambition to conquer international horizons? If "Conquering the Globe" became your compass, pointing you towards your global entrepreneurial North Star, I invite you to chart your thoughts with a review on Amazon.

Whether you believe this guide is worthy of five golden stars on the map or simply want to share your unique exploration insights, remember, it's the sincere feedback from fellow entrepreneurs like you that truly enriches this adventure.

Craving for more adventures and blueprints to entrepreneurial success? Discover the expanse of my writings on my Amazon author's page (**https://www.amazon.com/author/patrickhperrine**) and continue your journey towards international mastery. Together, let's inspire more souls to embark on their global ventures, one authentic review at a time.

Onwards and Beyond,
Patrick

About the Author

Patrick H. Perrine is a trailblazing author, mentor, and seasoned entrepreneur with a spirit that exemplifies the essence of entrepreneurship. From his humble beginnings as a paperboy in Minnesota to his emergence as a globally recognized industry leader, his journey epitomizes resilience and determination.

Fueled by an insatiable thirst for knowledge, Patrick opted for university over his senior high school year, setting the stage for his relentless pursuit of personal growth. His tenure with UpStart, an organization championing educational opportunities for first-generation Americans, ignited his lifelong commitment to empowering others, extending beyond business and into his early philanthropic endeavors.

In his twenties, Patrick served as a Founding Board member for The Point Foundation, the largest LGBTQ scholarship foundation today. His dedication to fostering inclusivity and aiding LGBTQ students in higher education continues to positively impact hundreds of lives.

Patrick's entrepreneurial journey took flight with myPartner.com, an online dating service that addressed a critical gap in the market. Recognized as one of the "Best Matchmakers" and "Most Innovative Online Dating Sites" by the iDate Industry, the venture earned a Certificate of Recognition issued by California Legislature Assemblyman Mark Leno. This marked Patrick's first step in a journey filled with identifying unique opportunities and delivering transformative solutions across industries from skincare to dog tech.

Despite the hurdles encountered, Patrick's determination only amplified. His passion for nurturing startups led him to establish Rincon Hill Advisors. During this period, he served as a Steering Committee member for StartOut, a leading nonprofit fostering queer entrepreneurship, and consulted with Fortune 500 companies like Berkshire Hathaway and Intuit.

Adding to his achievements as an entrepreneur, Patrick became an angel investor. His foresight led him to invest in promising startups like MisterB&B, the world's largest gay hotelier, and Roadster, the leading commerce platform for car buying. His dog tech venture, too, gained recognition, leading to his selection as a NGLCC Pitch Finalist and participant in the Seamless IoT Accelerator, earning a $100,000 investment offer as a program graduate.

Most recently, Patrick served as an Entrepreneur in Residence (EiR) with 500 StartUps, an organization committed to uplifting global economies through entrepreneurship. This role solidified his dedication to guiding and uplifting aspiring entrepreneurs.

With a total of six books to his credit, including recent works "Fail Fast, Recover Faster", "Ignite your Dream", and "Fueling the Fire", Patrick continues to share his journey and insights.

His writing reflects his unwavering commitment to guiding entrepreneurs through their unique journeys.

Patrick H. Perrine is more than a summary of his accomplishments. He stands as a testament to the power of determination, innovation, and a generous spirit. His contributions have been acknowledged in global press publications such as Forbes, Advocate, and Mirror, but his most profound impact lies in the lives of the entrepreneurs he's guided, inspired, and empowered.

Subscribe to my newsletter:

✉ https://www.patrickperrine.com

Also by Patrick H. Perrine

Your next adventure in entrepreneurship awaits! Choose your guidebook on Amazon (**https://www.amazon.com/author/patrickhperrine**) or **www.PatrickPerrine.com/books**, and ignite the spark that takes your venture to new heights. The future is yours to shape!

Unicorn Rising: Ascending to the Pinnacle of Entrepreneurship and the Billionaire's Club
Fueled by entrepreneurial dreams and the allure of the Unicorn Club? Patrick H. Perrine is your guide, offering an unparalleled roadmap set to be every entrepreneur's playbook.

"Unicorn Rising" emerges as the cornerstone of the *Be A Unicorn* series, laying the groundwork that "Conquering the Globe" and the other nine volumes build upon.

"Unicorn Rising" is more than a path to towering valuations; it's a compass to innovation, transformative leadership, and sustainable triumph. Dive into leadership's intricacies, the pulse of emerging tech, financial stewardship, and the essence of high-impact entrepreneurship.

However, this isn't a one-size-fits-all roadmap. While Patrick offers foundational wisdom and actionable tools, he accentuates the bespoke nature of each startup's odyssey. Whether you're an entrepreneurial novice or a battle-hardened veteran seeking to recalibrate strategies, this series becomes your beacon.

Embark, defy conventions, and with "Unicorn Rising", elevate to unparalleled entrepreneurial echelons.

Ignite Your Dream: The Quintessential Checklist for Aspiring Entrepreneurs

Ignite Your Dream: The Quintessential Checklist for Aspiring Entrepreneurs" by Patrick H. Perrine is an immersive guide lighting the path towards entrepreneurial success. This power-packed handbook propels you from dreaming to achieving with a carefully curated 100-step map. Dive into real-life entrepreneur stories, extract wisdom, and utilize actionable checklists.

This book transcends theoretical guidelines, providing a mentorship experience designed to turn dreams into reality. Ready to kindle your entrepreneurial spirit? "Ignite your Dream" is your step forward towards unlocking potential and achieving success in the exciting world of entrepreneurship.

Fail Fast, Recover Faster: Bouncing Back From Entrepreneurial Failure

Embrace failure and bounce back stronger with "Fail Fast, Recover Faster: Bouncing Back From Entrepreneurial Failure". It's your guidebook through the tumultuous journey of entrepreneurship, celebrating stumbles as stepping stones towards success. Dive into compelling tales of triumphant entrepreneurs, learn how to pivot rapidly, manage fallout, and convert setbacks into launchpads.

Discover strategies for repairing financial, relationship, and reputation damage, and see your failures as badges of resilience. This transformative book readies you to rebound from failure swiftly, turning your setbacks into your next entrepreneurial triumph. With "Fail Fast, Recover Faster", you're poised to harness your own unicorn moment and turn failure into a launching pad for success.

Fueling the Fire: Nurturing Resilience and Preventing Burnout in Entrepreneurship

In "Fueling the Fire: Nurturing Resilience and Preventing Burnout in Entrepreneurship," seasoned entrepreneur Patrick H. Perrine guides you through the entrepreneurial journey, sharing practical strategies for maintaining resilience and passion. Drawing from 20 years of startup experience, Perrine covers everything from ideation to acquisition.

Discover how to build a support system, manage your time effectively, cultivate a positive work culture, and align your work with your values. Whether you're an experienced entrepreneur or just beginning, "Fueling the Fire" is a must-read for maintaining balance and fulfillment in the dynamic world of entrepreneurship.